MW00379672

A Practical Scientific Guide to the Art and Science of Building Muscle

William D. Brink

Priming The Anabolic Environment

Priming The Anabolic Environment

Published by MuscleMag International
6465 Airport Road
Mississauga, Ontario
Canada L4V 1E4

Designed by Jackie Kydyk

10 9 8 7 6 5 4 3 2 1 Pbk.

Canadian Cataloging in Publication Data

Brink, William D., 1965–
    Priming the anabolic environment: a practical and
scientific guide to the art and science of building muscle

Includes bibliographical references and index.
ISBN 1-55210-003-0

    1.Bodybuilding. I. Title.
GV546.5.B75 1996   646.7'5   C96-900203-3

Distributed in Canada by MuscleMag International
6465 Airport Road
Mississauga, Ontario
Canada L4V 1E4

Distributed in the United States by
MuscleMag International
(Swan Screening)
1789 South Park Avenue
Buffalo, New York
USA 14220
Printed in Canada.
Parts of this book have been reproduced with permission of
MuscleMag International.

To Michelle, the best friend and companion a man could ask for, and a damn fine editor too.

This book is not intended as medical advice, nor is it offered for use in the diagnosis of any health condition or as a substitute for medical treatment and/or counsel. Its purpose is to explore advanced topics on sports nutrition and exercise. All data are for information only. Use of any of the programs within this book is at the sole risk and choice of the reader.

Thanks to Bob Kennedy and Johnny Fitness at *MuscleMag International* for your continued support and advice.

Table of Contents – Priming The Anabolic Environment

Priming The Anabolic Environment – *Table of Contents*

Read what the experts and stars of bodybuilding had to say about Will Brink's new book.

Vic Richards. <u>World's most massive bodybuilder:</u>
"Will Brink is one of the most knowledgeable writers and trainers in bodybuilding today. He uses science, experience and common sense in his approach to gaining muscle. I highly recommend this book."

Craig Licker. <u>'94 NPC National/USA champ and IFBB pro :</u>
"I gave Will Brink the name 'the secret weapon' and it stuck. His knowledge of training, diet and supplementation was invaluable to my assault on the Nationals and USA. If you can't train with him in person as I did, this book is the next best thing. There is something in this book for everybody who seeks to add muscle, lose fat or improve health."

Craig Titus. <u>Bodybuilding superstar, '96 USA Overall winner and IFBB Pro:</u>
"Will has a knack for taking complicated information and presenting it in a straightforward and easy-to-read format. Bodybuilding is more of a science than an art today, and in this book you have the science of modern bodybuilding covered by one of the very best trainers in the business."

Kevin Peterson.<u>'94 ANBC USA champ and natural pro:</u>
"When Will Brink gives advice I listen. He has helped me out more than a few times, and that help paid off in a big way at the ANBC USA. Natural bodybuilders have different needs from athletes who use drugs, and Will knows how to push a person's genetics to the max, drugs or no drugs.

Dallas Clouatre. <u>Ph.D. Nutritional researcher and the author of the books, *Anti- Fat Nutrients* and *The Health Benefits of HCA*:</u>
"Priming The Anabolic Environment *should be of interest to anyone who is striving to achieve peak performance in athletics and/or bodybuilding. Will Brink's chapters provide some of the smartest advice to be found on these topics. The book was written by a man who has seen it all and then distilled his experience for the benefit of the readers. This material is always practical; it is supported by real science and has been proven in real-life competitions. Will's easy and accessible writing style makes all this information sit lightly with the reader."*

Edwin Worthy B.Sc. M.D. <u>MIT researcher and avid bodybuilder:</u>
"I have always been impressed with Will Brink's scope of knowledge of nutrition and training, which I have relied on for years to improve my workouts and overall health. I have personally put much of the information in this book to use in my own workouts and I can honestly say that my gains in muscle have never been better. I plan to get the first copy of this book for my library."

Fred Bigo. <u>Winner of the '94 CanAm Bodybuilding Championship:</u>
"Before I met Will Brink, training and nutrition were pretty much a hit or miss thing for me. After his advice and help, much of which can be found in this book, the results have been right on target every time. A 'must read' book if there ever was one."

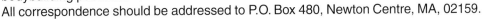

William Brink is a contributing consultant, columnist and writer for *MuscleMag International*. He has been published in over 13 countries on various topics relating to bodybuilding and health and fitness. Will graduated from Harvard University with a concentration in the natural sciences. He is a well-known trainer who has worked with many high-level athletes ranging from professional bodybuilders and fitness contestants to Olympic hammer throwers and professional golfers. He is a consultant to several supplement companies and a judge for the National Physique Committee (NPC) and Ms. Fitness USA.

Will has lectured on the benefits of weight training and sports nutrition at conventions in New York, Los Angeles, and the Metro Sport convention in Boston. In addition to his own writing, he has co-authored articles with several notable scientists, such as Dr. Udo Erasmus, Dallas Clouatre Ph.D., and Edwin Worthy B.Sc., M.D., on various subjects relating to health and fitness. Through Brink Training Systems (BTS) he continues to assist many of the country's top athletes by means of seminars, phone consultation, and writing in *MuscleMag International* and other health and bodybuilding publications.

All correspondence should be addressed to P.O. Box 480, Newton Centre, MA, 02159.

You now hold in your hands what could be one of the most useful books you have ever read for gaining permanent muscle. Some of the sections in this book might be a bit too technical for some people, while for others it will be an easy read. I hope it will be an interesting book for everyone regardless of background.

Not every part concerns itself just with building muscle. Marketing your hard-earned muscle and/or showing that muscle to its best advantage at a bodybuilding contest – if you decide to compete – are also covered. If you are already a seasoned competitor, there should still be a few tips and pointers that will help at your next competition. It is a shame how many good bodybuilders there are in the world who don't "make it" because they are unable to market themselves correctly or show their physique to its best advantage when onstage.

You won't find absolute recommendations on exercises you must do or foods you must eat 27 seconds after your last set of squats on the night of a full moon over the body of a dead chicken! You will get all the information you need from the chapters on nutrition and training to optimize your anabolic environment without finding yourself chained to the inflexible and unrealistic practices that are so common in many of today's mail-order courses. In many ways gaining muscle is far simpler than you think, and in other ways it is far more complex than most people realize.

This book allows for a good amount of flexibility because the rules of acquiring new muscle are not carved in stone as some "experts" or people trying to sell you something would have you believe. Armed with solid foundational knowledge, you will be able to come up with your own formula (while keeping within important dietary and training parameters) for gaining more muscle than you probably thought you ever would.

You will notice that I have not written a routine for every bodypart or told you exactly how you should split up those bodyparts. I have put in what I have found to be some of the most effective routines for the muscles you should spend the majority of your time training – i.e. legs, back and chest. These three areas are truly the "growth centers" of the body, but more on that later. I have also included a chapter on calves – because almost everyone can use more calves – and a short chapter on arm-training because people waste so much time on

IFBB pros Chris Cormier, David Dearth, Aaron Baker, Vince Taylor and Lee Priest.

their arms. In many cases they either end up looking like a legless gorilla, or else they overtrain their biceps and triceps so severely that those small bodyparts don't grow much. My favorite bodypart chapter is the one on calf-training. If you can survive those workouts you will add size to your calves, period. As for how you should split up your bodyparts, as long as you train the correct number of days per week, stay in the gym the right amount of time, and stick roughly to the number of sets that are recommended for each bodypart, the decision is really up to you.

How a person splits up his bodyparts depends on many factors, such as the number of days he plans to train, how long he has been training, if he is trying to bring up a lagging bodypart, or just has certain bodyparts he either loves or hates to train in the same workout. Within reason, changing around your bodypart split is not going to determine whether or not you become Mr. Olympia or Mr. Pencil- neck. It just is not that important. If you like to train chest and shoulders together, by all means do it that way. Personally, I hate to train chest and shoulders in the same workout, but that's what makes horse-racing. What is important is that you train few days per week (three or four is best), get out of the gym promptly (preferably under an hour), don't overdo the aerobics, and get home as fast as possible to eat plenty of high-quality food and the correct supplements.

When training three days per week, I have found doing chest and back on Monday, legs on Wednesday, and shoulders, arms and calves on Friday to be the most effective. If I'm training four days per week, the split is a bit different: chest and arms on Monday, back on Tuesday, legs on Thursday, and shoulders and calves on Friday. Of course, the schedule would have to change anyway after a few months because of the boredom factor. You do change your split around every few months, don't you?

The biggest training mistake you could make is to follow the six-day-per-week, twice-a-day routine of some genetically gifted, juiced-to-the-hilt, nonworking pro bodybuilder you see in the magazines. Of all the advice I have ever given to some of the highest-level competitive bodybuilders, the idea of doing fewer sets and spending fewer days in the gym

Flex Wheeler

probably accounts for half of the success I have had getting already large people even larger. Anyway, I am getting ahead of myself and have given away half the book in the introduction, so I will say no more about training. Read the rest of the book and you should find the answers to any questions that might have been evoked by this brief discussion.

Charles Clairmonte

bodybuilders can't seem to get enough when it comes to talking or reading about steroids, and yes, I would sell more books if I rattled off high-tech steroid stacks till the reader bulged at the eyes from excitement, but that is not the type of book I wanted to write. This book contains information that all athletes can benefit from whether they use drugs or not. If you follow what I have written in the following chapters you will gain muscle. If you add drugs (at your own risk physically and legally) you will obviously add even more muscle. My only interest in steroids and other drugs as they relate to this book is to put down on paper my personal views and opinions on the subject (see chapter 7) and give you some guidelines to keep you, the reader, healthy (see chapters 8-9) if that reader – you? – insists on using steroids. Other than that, I have not gone into much additional detail on the topic of drugs in bodybuilding. I find manipulating the body into growing muscle by way of nutrition, training and supplements a far more challenging and interesting pursuit. I hope the reader will find it equally interesting.

Finally, you will notice a single theme throughout this book. It is the all-important idea that whatever you do to improve your muscle mass should also improve, or at least not de-grade, your health. Muscles are great. Health is still more important. If you don't agree, take 10 Anadrol a day, get as big as a house, and tell your friends to send me a picture of your huge self after you pass away. If you do agree that your good health is at least as important as increasing your muscle mass, then you have definitely come to the right place and purchas-ed the correct book. I have worked with some of the finest athletes in the world, and most of them were fairly healthy people (with some admittedly unhealthful practices). I have also known many a skinny gym rat who did not look as if he had more than a few months to live from his bad eating habits and year-round drug use. Don't think to get larger you necessarily have to compromise your health to the extreme. The only thing worse than death is having nothing to live for. Make the most of life, but don't lose it in the process.

In this book you will find all the inform-ation you need to make the most of your genetics. I am not saying you will go from a string bean to Mr. Olympia, but if you have at least average genetics for making muscle you can definitely add new size to your frame by closely following what I have spent years re-searching to put down on paper for the reader. As for steroids and other drugs, you might be disappointed to find I do not devote a great deal of space to the subject. In my view it is a topic that has been done to death. Sure,

– Will Brink

Ronnie Coleman

Chapter One

The Business of Bodybuilding

"Making It" in the Fitness Industry

It seems only reasonable that we begin this book with the business aspect of the sport and lifestyle which is bodybuilding. No matter how fantastic your body is, if you can't make any money from it you will not reap the full rewards of your hard work. The fitness industry

David Dearth

is big business. Bodybuilding, which is certainly part of the fitness industry, can also be big business for people who successfully tap into this growing market. Yeah, I know, the term "fitness" is sort of a whiny and wimpy word to us bodybuilders, but it is here to stay, so we have to deal with it. The word "fitness" doesn't exactly come to mind when you are lying on the floor seeing stars from a set of high-rep squats. Unfortunately bodybuilders have always been their own worst enemy when it comes to tapping into this lucrative field. Have you ever wondered why some bodybuilders (who might or might not have won major contests) do so well for themselves, while others are never heard from again? Inside and outside the fitness industry, including the bodybuilding sector, most bodybuilders are seen as flaky, rude and self-absorbed. Is this reputation deserved, or do they just get a bad rap?

Many bodybuilders, after winning an important competition, think all they have to do is wait for the phone to start ringing off the hook with million-dollar offers and huge magazine spreads. Sure, a few superstars get immediate attention afterwards, but this is the exception, not the rule. Winning the major shows is only half the battle to becoming successful in the incredibly competitive fitness market. A lot of bodybuilders who have never competed do better than the ones who do compete. If you want to make it, you had better take it to the world – don't wait for the world to come to you (i.e. you have to hustle your ass off!).

In this chapter I am going to relate a few experiences I have had (so you can decide for yourself if the reputation is deserved), give you some tips on things not to do (so you won't encounter the same pitfalls), and offer a few pointers that will help in your quest to become a well-liked, respected and ultimately successful bodybuilder. This is not going to be some sort of "how to get rich from bodybuilding" business plan. If I had that information, I would be sitting on a beach, collecting interest payments while reading a muscle mag, instead of plunking away on my word processor in freezing New England!

Ronnie Coleman

Experiences

#1 The rude experience:

Last year I judged a fairly large regional competition. At the show I recognized one of the competitors as a good friend of a good friend of mine. He recognized me also. He ended up doing well for himself, winning his class and just barely missing the overall. Although he did not win the whole show, I thought he had a great deal of potential to go further in bodybuilding. I called him up a week later to tell him that, and to offer my services if he needed any help. Before I could get the compliment out of my mouth, he said: "I can't believe you didn't give me the whole show. All my friends said I should have won. You are a f***ing sh**y judge. I think I will call the head judge up and tell him he sucks too." Needless to say, I didn't offer him any help.

#2 The flaky experience:

A bodybuilder telephoned me one day to tell me he had just won a show, and asked me if I could possibly do a small piece on him as he was in good shape and wanted some publicity. I told him I would be happy to meet him at his gym to take some pictures, and if they turned out well, I would do a short article. We made the appointment for the following week. With my camera loaded, I drove about 45 minutes to meet him. He never showed up. He called me a few days later to say he had slept through our appointment and asked if we could make another. I told him I did not have the time to waste, and if he wanted a story done he could come to my gym at a time that was convenient to me. He never called me back.

#3 The rude, unprofessional experience:

A pro bodybuilder who shall remain nameless (because he is about five times my size) kept blowing me off for an interview. I phoned him four times, but he never returned the calls. I left messages with his girlfriend, his roommate, and on his answering machine, but no answer. Finally I bumped into him at a bodybuilding show, and asked him if he wanted publicity (which is obviously important for business), why he didn't return my phone calls. He replied, "Man, I was just so burnt out after that last show I did, I didn't feel like talking to anybody for a while, but I planned to get back to you. I guess I forgot to call." After that I didn't "feel" like calling him again.

Unfortunately I could write a whole book of these stories. I have heard similar tales from other writers, photographers, editors and contest promoters. We want to make these guys and gals famous, but do they want it too? It would not appear from this unprofessional behavior that they have any interest in succeeding. I don't want you to think all bodybuilders are like this because they are not. I have also had plenty of good experiences, just not as many as I would like. Hey, most of my best friends are bodybuilders, but I wouldn't trust them as far as I could throw them to show up on time for a simple lunch appointment. If the sport and the business of bodybuilding are going to flourish in the dog-eat-dog 1990s and beyond, we had better get our collective acts together, or we will

Jeffrey Snyder

be left in the dust of the ever-advancing armies of smiling, stair- stepping, bun-firming, "fitness" people! Ugh!

Below is a short list of strategies to adopt and behaviors to avoid. If you want to learn more about business in general, read a few books on marketing, management and business, or take some courses. Believe me when I tell you, bodybuilding (as with all businesses) is about marketing yourself to the fullest. Big muscles don't hurt either.

Behavior to Avoid

Never, ever, show bad sportsmanship at contests. Don't rely on family and friends, who can't possibly be objective, to tell you where you should have placed. Competitors who storm offstage, smash trophies or call officials names, nail their own coffin shut in the eyes of promoters, sponsors and judges. This advice also goes for people attending the show. This is the place to make friends, business contacts and good impressions, not show off the latest tank

top and bad attitude. I am constantly amazed by the number of bodybuilders who complain about the lack of respect they receive, while wearing cutoff spandex shorts and a T-shirt that reads, "Get big or get out of town." At all times, whether at the gym, on the street or at a contest, you are an ambassador for the great sport and lifestyle that is bodybuilding. We know we are the hardest-training, most dedicated athletes in the world, but that does not mean everyone else knows it, or cares for that matter. Create a professional appearance of yourself, and it will pay off.

Be patient with people. I know it is hard to keep a straight face with stupid...er, uninformed people when they say things like "What do you mean I can't work the same muscle seven days in a row?" or "I thought bagels were loaded with protein." And my personal favorite, "I have only 23 sets left on the Smith machine, but you can have it when I'm done." They don't mean any harm. They just don't know any better. I too have been caught being short tempered, but I am quick to do damage control. People with short tempers and bad attitudes will have their reputation precede them wherever they go. Once you have been tagged as someone with a bad attitude, it is virtually impossible to shake the rap. Many of today's top bodybuilders have a reputation in the business as having a bad attitude and are considered hard to work with, and they pay the price with less press and fewer opportunities, which translates into less money in the long run.

Be prepared — "knowledge is power!" There has never been a truer statement. I can't tell you how many times I have seen some pencil-thin, arm-chair-scientist, better-than-thou physiologist type talk down to, through or over the head of a bodybuilder because the bodybuilder had not bothered to do his homework. You should read everything you can get your hands on that pertains to your sport, business, etc. Some bodybuilders are not the brightest bulb in the lamp, but many are smart people who just don't have the knowledge or scientific vocabulary they need to defend themselves against the onslaught of garbage information that is so prevalent in the "fitness" industry. Moral of the story? Never stop learning! You can never know too much, only too little.

Strategies For Success

Besides the obvious stuff (e.g. professional attitude, good appearance), there are a few small things you can do that have a large impact on how people will perceive you.

(1) Have business cards made up. You should never have to scramble for a pen and paper when a business opportunity requires you to give your phone number. Don't get cheap ones either! Good business cards say something about you, and leave a lasting impression. I can tell you that cheap business cards often end up in the garbage.

(2) Be assertive and persistent, but don't be pushy and irritating. There is a fine line between these two strategies.

(3) Always, always, always return phone calls promptly, follow up phone calls with a short letter, and follow up letters with a short phone call. Making clear that you are enthusiastic (but not pushy) is priority number one. Personally, I will not even consider working with anyone who doesn't return phone calls promptly, show up on time for appointments, or practice basic business etiquette. I know many people at all levels of the bodybuilding and fitness industry who feel the same way.

(4) Always have photos on hand. Get body shots done when you look your best – head shots too. Have both done by a good photographer. If someone asks you for a photo, you should be prepared to supply one immediately. Many fine bodybuilders have missed potential job opportunities because of this oversight.

(5) If you place well in a show, or don't even compete but think you have the body and the look the magazines might be interested in, send pictures! The magazines are always looking for new talent. Send your picture with a well-written and proofread cover letter. Follow it up with a phone call (see strategy number four). Muscles are in! Send your pictures to modeling agencies. Approach local contest promoters for guest posing. Don't fear rejection. Fear failure. It is stupefying how lazy bodybuilders can be about promoting themselves. Being able to work out intensely is only part of it. You must promote yourself intensely too, no matter what type of job you have or want to have.

(6) Last but not least, if you are not good at promoting yourself, pay someone who is! No one can be good at everything. (I am particularly bad at math!) All sports figures and entertainment personalities have someone helping them with marketing themselves. It doesn't have to cost you a million dollars either (though some people do pay that much). You can pay someone a hundred bucks a month to do some of the work for you and help you come up with new ideas.

Conclusion

These recommendations could be used by anyone in any business. They are just good guidelines based on common sense that can be applied specifically to bodybuilding. Put them to good use and you could be rewarded handsomely. Train heavy, eat big and market yourself to the fullest.

Chapter Two
The Successful Competitor

Winning bodybuilding shows is more than strict dieting, and being successful in bodybuilding is more than just winning shows. If taking copious amounts of (ahem) supplements and dieting strictly were all there was to winning contests, the process of obtaining victory would be an easy one. Unfortunately far too many competitive bodybuilders seem to believe this is the case, only to see their hopes go up in smoke when their name is not called out for a trophy. Avoiding the obvious (i.e. correct dieting, training, supplementation, etc.), we are going to address in this chapter the most common mistakes bodybuilders make leading up to a competition and what they can do to avoid them. Though small individually, these all-too-common mistakes can combine (a.k.a. negative synergism) to be the downfall of a potential winner.

I can't tell you how many times I have been judging a bodybuilding contest only to have the judge sitting next to me whisper something like "Hey, if this guy could pose better and had tanned more, he could have taken this show easily." The fact is , the athlete who wins the contest is rarely the one with the best genetics. More often the winner is the person who on that day presents the best total package, including correct and even skin color, good posing and confident stage presence. From the pros to the local shows attention to detail wins out over genetics. Successful competitors such as Lee Labrada, Porter Cottrell and Vince Taylor are perfect examples of bodybuilders who regularly beat larger men using this strategy. They are "total package" competitors.

Obviously your number one priority is to be ripped, huge and symmetrical, but if the guy standing next to you is in equally good condition, and has also done his homework, you can kiss that trophy goodbye because it will be on his mantelpiece instead of yours.

Porter Cottrell bags another pro title.

Physique Productions Presents This Award To The Winner Of Night Of The Champions XV Saturday, May 22, 1993 Beacon Theater New York City

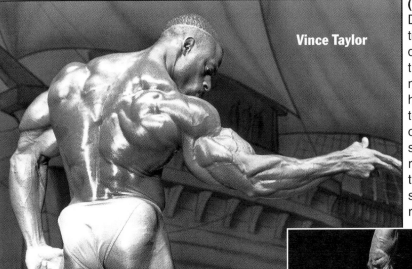

Vince Taylor

(1) Keep an open mind: Don't be afraid to try different training methods, especially during the off-season. Contrary to what many "experts" might tell you (because they have a course of some kind to sell), there is no "one and only" correct way to train. Try supersetting, giant sets, high reps, low reps, etc. Shock the muscle. Don't bore yourself and your muscles into a rut.

Former Mr. Olympia Frank Zane.

Remember, it's all right to be beaten by a better competitor, but it's not all right to be beaten by your own mistakes. The sad thing is, I have occasionally had competitors throw obscenities at me (not a career-enhancing tactic) after a show because they didn't place where they felt they should have. So what if their posing suit looked more like diapers, and I wondered if Pro Tan had been outlawed in their state, but what striations! Seriously, here are some pointers and suggestions that should see you several placings higher – assuming you are in shape – at your next outing. Who knows? Maybe you will find yourself in in the winner's circle.

(2) Monitor your progress carefully: Start your precontest preparations early (14-16 weeks minimum). Weigh yourself every day. To maintain maximum muscle mass, you should lose no more than one to one and a half pounds per week during your precontest phase. Have your fat tested with calipers or hydrostatic weighing every two to four weeks. Write down everything you eat. Using a calorie-counting book and a calculator, you should know exactly

Dorian Yates and Kevin Levrone at the 1994 Mr. Olympia. Yates scored his third win.

how many calories, grams of protein, carbohydrates and fat you take in each day, plus sodium, potassium and other dietary variables that can affect your precontest preparation. I use a computer program that figures all this out. I highly recommend it, though the job definitely can be done with a calculator and a calorie-counting book that you can find in any book store. Believe me, every top competitor or his trainer can tell you how many calories or grams of protein he ate for any given day. With few exceptions people who eat and train by "feel" precontest rarely get to "feel" the weight of a trophy in their hand. Make no mistake about it – bodybuilding is a science. The fewer unknown variables you have to deal with the better.

(3) Be familiar with the judging criteria: Some time ago a bodybuilder asked me to help him with his routine for his first competition. I said, "Sure, I will help you with your routine, but what about your mandatory poses?" To which he replied, "What mandatory poses?" Would you show up to play in a football game without knowing the rules? I should hope not! Contrary to what some people might think, there are very specific rules of conduct and performance dur-

ing a bodybuilding competition. You should know them all by heart. Unfortunately more than a few competitors place lower than they should because of their ignorance of the rules. Ask a successful competitor or local judge to help you. Attend shows in your area and study them carefully.

(4) Enter a warmup show a few weeks prior to the contest you are preparing for: For people who have limited experience, or have never competed before, this is a great way to work out the jitters and kinks in your posing. You should not go with the intention of winning, but to gain invaluable experience for the competition you have set your sights on. Consider it practice. Doing this will also help you to become familiar with the judging criteria. The competitors I have worked with found this tactic extremely helpful. Don't do anything special for this show (such as carb deplete) that will detract from your ability to peak for the important contest ahead.

(5) Practice, practice, practice: Start posing seriously – 30 to 40 minutes daily – no less than six weeks prior to the contest. No matter how fantastic you look, if you can't show your physique in the best possible manner the judges will never know how good you are. What good is being in great condition if you can't pose worth a damn? This is probably the most common mistake you will see at local or regional events – and a few pro shows. Watch tapes of great posers such as Shawn Ray, Lee Lebrada and Vince Taylor, or other bodybuilders you think pose well. Have a choreographer or friend help you if you are not naturally good at posing. Make sure the music you pick reflects your physique and your personality. Have a friend videotape your routine and mandatory poses, and have other experienced competitors critique it until you get it down perfectly. Design your poses so that your best bodyparts are emphasized and your weaker bodyparts are less prominent. Smile at all times, and don't let your guard down by relaxing muscles, letting your stomach hang out or talking too much. Even if you are not in the front lineup posing, the judges are still looking at you, and they don't

like to see that basketball some bodybuilders call a stomach hanging over their suit. Practice posing in front of real live people and not just the mirror. Posing practice has the added benefit of improving muscle separation and overall hardness. Far too many bodybuilders leave their posing until the last minute, if they do it at all, and pay the price.

A second advantage to posing regularly before your contest is the development of endurance. Posing is hard work! You will be amazed how hard it is to pose for 30 minutes straight. Too often one sees a bodybuilder doubled over and gasping for air in the lineup – not exactly what the judges are looking for!

(6) Ask people you trust for criticism and use it: How many times have you heard the guy (or gal) in your gym with no legs, no tan, and a huge Budweiser tattoo on his back say, "I'm gonna win the whole show, man!" When it is over, he is always the guy who tells you he was robbed (because his friends and family

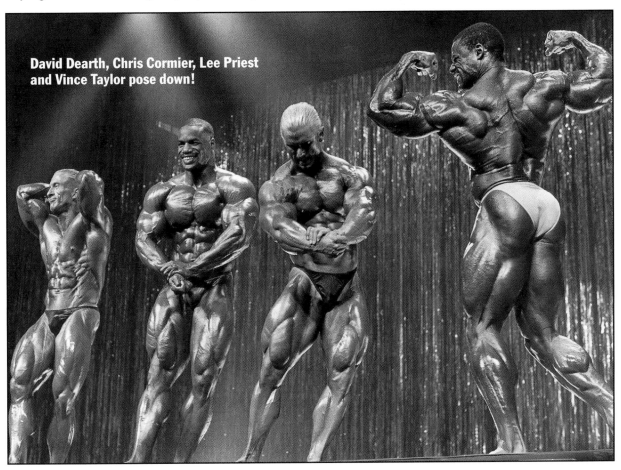

David Dearth, Chris Cormier, Lee Priest and Vince Taylor pose down!

Boston's Mike Matarazzo.

matter), as they cannot and will not be objective. The most important people to ask are the judges. Regardless of how you feel about the placings, you probably won't be able to get your mother on the judging panel next year, so the judges are the people to ask. Strangely enough, I have been to many types of competitive events (gymnastics, skating, aerobics, etc.) and noticed a long line of competitors waiting for feedback after the contest. In my years of judging bodybuilding shows, I have never seen more than a few competitors show up for feedback after each contest. Talk about missing out on good advice!

(8) Experiment with tanning products, and tan no matter what color you are: Correct skin color is essential. It is amazing how much proper skin preparation can affect the outcome of a contest. Most newcomers fail to tan enough and/or use enough tanning products or use them correctly. Having just witnessed the '95 Arnold Classic, I can assure you that a few of the pros make that mistake too. Without naming names, there were several pros at this show (as there are at every contest) who were in great shape, but were held back by their skin color – i.e. no base tan under Pro Tan, blotchy spots, missing spots, etc. Everyone is different and will need more or less tanning. The warmup competition that is recommended (see # 4) is a perfect opportunity to experiment and find the correct skin color for you. Don't wait until the day of the event to find out you didn't tan enough or apply enough coats of Pro Tan. Though black men might not need the color, tanning tightens the skin (making you look harder), helps eliminate fluid from under your skin, and gives a healthier glow to the skin come show time.

You must have a good natural base tan, with all your body hair shaved off before you apply a tanning product, or you will look a yellowish orange onstage, not unlike a carrot. When applying a tanning product, make sure to have no streaks, blotchy spots or missing spots. Don't forget to apply it to your face! Some

told him so). People like this obviously don't ask for feedback, or when they do, they don't listen to a word anyone says to them. They have already convinced themselves they are the greatest thing since Arnold and Sergio, and if you tell them differently, they never ask your advice again. They have a knack for searching out people who tell them what they want to hear, and avoid people who tell them what they *need* to hear. They will always look the same because they are too closed minded and egotistical (really a fragile ego) to take good advice. Don't be one of these people. Seek out trainers, competitors or friends you can trust and use their feedback to your advantage. Walk softly and carry a big trophy!

(7) Always ask judges for feedback after a competition no matter where you place: If you win, you will want to know what you can do in the future to win bigger shows. If you don't win, you will want to know what you can improve to do better at the same event in the future. Don't ever rely on friends and family to tell you what went wrong (or what went right for that

competitors (especially women) have the odd habit of coming onstage with dark body and a white face. This practice is very distracting and serves only to lose points for the competitor. Though there are several high-quality tanning products on the market, the Jan Tana tanning cream and competition oil work well for most people. Three coats of the tanning cream the night before and one coat the day of the contest (on top of a good base tan) usually does the trick.

(9) Apply oil correctly: All the advice above for tanning also applies here. Too much oil makes you look smooth (jelly doughnut syndrome), and too little makes you look flat. The oil must be even all over the body. Spots most often missed: middle of back, glutes, inner

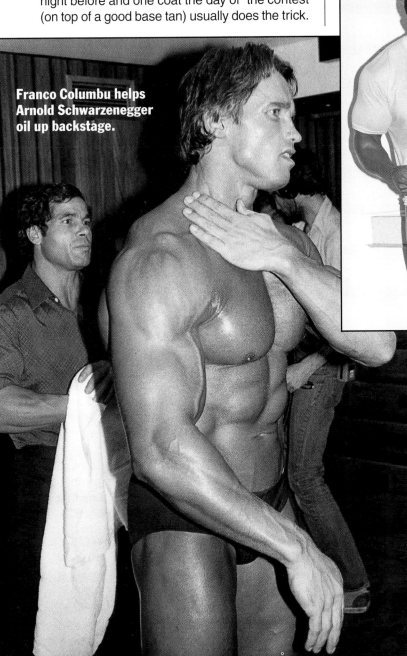

Franco Columbu helps Arnold Schwarzenegger oil up backstage.

Legendary competitor Bertil Fox.

thighs, armpits and side of lats, under chin and back of neck. People have different ways of applying oil, but this is my personal favorite. First apply a light coat and rub thoroughly into the skin. Apply a second light coat on top of the first coat and check for evenness. You can rub the second coat lightly to correct uneven spots, but do not rub it deeply into skin.

(10) Develop a good stage presence: Winners are not winners just because they have the best body. Winners project their desire to win at the judges and the audience. Performers in the visual arts – dancers, actors, singers – know the importance of projection. Bodybuilding is a vis-

Tony Pearson, Mohamed Makkawy, Lee Haney and Jusup Wilkosz

seen on television. Did they have a certain quality above and beyond their great body that told you they were going to win? I bet they did.

Sometimes you have to spend weeks with a person just trying to help him develop a better stage presence. For some people it comes naturally, but for others it is a learned skill just like any other. At the local level judges take into account the nervousness of inexperienced bodybuilders, but above the local level poor stage presence is a real detriment that does not go unnoticed. It is your job to convince people (i.e. judges, audience, media, etc.) that you are a winner no matter where you place. Your body language and facial expression should say, "I am here to do battle and I can compete with the best this show has to offer." Don't be cocky or try to push other competitors aside. Just deliver the goods with confidence and class.

(11) Be courteous in defeat: Though slightly different, this is similar to number 10. Remember, you can't win 'em all. Arnold, Yates, Haney and Flex Wheeler have all been defeated at one time or another. Believe me, it does not go unnoticed by magazine editors, promoters, judges and the audience when a bodybuilder shows some class in defeat. A winning attitude regardless of where you place is what separates the true professional from the amateur. It is easy to be gracious when you're winning, but graciousness in defeat shows a great deal more character.

(12) Market yourself constantly and strive to have a good reputation: You are not competing just to win the contest, but to get a reputation (hopefully a good one!) and to be known. It is not uncommon for a third- or fourth-place finisher to get more attention and press than the winner. Marketing yourself fully is just as important, not to mention profitable, as winning any competition. The subject of marketing was covered in chapter one, so we will not go into great detail on the subject here. Simply, you need to avoid at all costs a reputation for being a poor loser (see # 11), hard to work with or unreliable, as a bad reputation will follow you everywhere you go.

Lenda Murray and Laura Creavalle always show class in competition.

ual sport. Your ability to project your confidence, poise and determination to succeed is almost as important as the body you present. Think about the winners of some shows you have gone to or

(13) Suit and hair: Make sure you are well groomed (as in no five o'clock shadow), and have a tight, neat hair style. Your suit should fit tightly around the body, especially the back side. The Pampers diaper look really kills your symmetry! Remember to account for lost inches from your waist, hips and glutes when you order the suit. If you have short legs and a long torso or a wide waist, make sure the suit sits high up on the thighs. If you have large glutes (a polite way of saying big butt), use a dark-colored fabric for your suit. Don't just pick your favorite color and make a posing suit out of it. It might look great on you as a shirt, but could be the wrong color to highlight or hide aspects of your physique. #@*& happens (a.k.a. Murphy's law), so buy two or three suits just in case something happens to one of them.

Besides a high degree of muscle mass, good symmetry and low bodyfat, the successful competitive bodybuilder
(1) keeps an open mind when training;
(2) monitors his/her progress constantly and correctly;
(3) knows the judging criteria;
(4) gets experience by entering a warmup show;
(6) has a strong enough ego to ask for criticism and uses it to improve his physique;
(7) gets the necessary feedback from judges;
(8) has the correct amount of tanning product over a good base tan;
(9) has the correct amount of oil on, evenly distributed over the entire body;
(10) has great stage presence;
(11) is as courteous in defeat as in victory;
(12) constantly markets himself and strives to have a good reputation;
(13) has a great-fitting, physique-complementing posing suit and hair style.

In the end it is not just the body that wins the contest or earns the respect of those involved in the sport, but the entire package you present. Even with some genetic limitations you will be amazed how far you can go if you strive to be a "total package" competitor. This "package" of yours, besides helping you win contests, is what will determine your marketability and ultimately your success. If you put the recom-

mendations and suggestions in this chapter to good use, and are lucky enough to have been born with the right parents (sorry, can't help you there), you could have the trophy of your dreams and all the potential goodies that go with it. Of course, I can't guarantee your success, but stranger things have happened.

Andreas Munzer was one of the freakiest competitors of all time.

Chapter Three
Priming the Anabolic Environment

Bodybuilding is a curious sport. One person can train his butt off and grow very little muscle, while another person will do virtually everything wrong and put on mass without trouble. Of course, the first group of trainers is far more common than the second, but these easy gainers do exist. What is the difference between these two groups? Genetics! People vary widely in their ability to secrete and utilize hormones, both anabolic and catabolic. They vary in the number of muscle cells they have in a given area, and the number of fat cells they have also. Unfortunately you probably can't affect the number of fat and muscle cells you have (only their size changes), but you can affect the way your body produces certain hormones and how it utilizes them. Genetic limitations are dramatically altered by steroids, but the same rule of genetics still applies.

Some people can use extremely small amounts of anabolics and make good gains, while others will use enough testosterone to kill an elephant (or at least make his hair fall out) and will still get little result. The moral of the story? Drugs or no drugs, you can't escape your genetics. What you can do, whether you have used drugs or not, is optimize the anabolic environment of your body to make the most of your genes.

The three major anabolic hormones of the body are growth hormone, insulin and testosterone. Which one of the three is the most anabolic is still being debated. These hormones work and interact in an extremely complex fashion. They are released by various feedback mechanisms that are dependent on the levels of yet more hormones and other physiological variables. For example, there are glucagon, insulin-like growth factor (IGF-I), luteinizing

Paul Dillett, Kevin Levrone, Dorian Yates and Shawn Ray square off at the 1994 Mr. Olympia.

hormone (LH), gonadotropin-releasing hormone (GnRH), thyroid hormones and many, many more.

I just wanted to point out briefly how incredibly complicated this topic can get, but for this book we will concern ourselves with the three main anabolic hormones and what can be done to stimulate them – if they can be stimulated at all. I don't want to fool you into thinking I am the end-all expert on hormones and hormone manipulation. I spend a considerable amount of time researching the subject, but the complexity of the subject matter is almost incomprehensible at times. If I understood everything there was to know about hormones, I would be a rich man. There is a great deal of research going on in the field of endocrinology (the study of hormones and how they affect muscle mass, fat, etc.), but it will be some years before anyone can claim to understand it all, and a few more years to find people who can understand that guy! Luckily for us, we do know a fair amount about how the body reacts to certain variables – diet, training, rest – and how to alter these variables to achieve the desired result within the limitations of one's genetics.

Superpro Michael Francois

Training

Different types of training have different results as to which of the three anabolic hormones are secreted or utilized in the highest concentrations. Testosterone is released in its highest concentrations using heavy loads (5-10 RM) using longer rest periods of three to five minutes* between sets. Growth hormone is released at a peak using slightly higher reps (10-12+) and short rest periods of 30 to 60 seconds. (1) Insulin is much more responsive to dietary factors than it is to training. How the insulin is utilized (and when) is a combination of training and diet. I feel that higher rep ranges of 15-20 make muscle cell receptors more accepting of insulin (which forces glucose and amino acids into the muscle) following a workout. This is only my opinion, and it is based on experience, not research, so take it for what it's worth. Regardless of rep range, muscle cells are most receptive to glucose (primarily derived from dietary carbohydrates)

driven into the muscle cells by insulin following a high-intensity workout. Thus postworkout is the best time to consume a carbohydrate drink. We will get more into the subject of glucose, carbohydrates and insulin later in the chapter when we discuss diet.

Extremely important to know is the exercise selection for growth hormone and testosterone (and possibly insulin reactivity) that has been shown to elicit the greatest response. Exercises that demand the most muscle tissue – multijoint exercises such as squats, bent rows and dips – have a far greater effect on the anabolic drive (i.e. hormones released during exercise) than do isolation exercises. This is why people who rely on exercises like one-arm cable pushdowns and concentration curls fail to add an ounce of muscle unless they are using drugs to counter their poor training habits. It's the guys who grit their teeth and sweat buckets during squats, bent rows and deadlifts who make the serious gains. Don't get me wrong. Isolation exercises are important at

A pair of the biggest biceps in the sport belongs to Ronnie Coleman.

certain times, but relying on them totally, as we have all seen many young bodybuilders doing, will leave you skinnier than Pee-Wee Herman.

If muscle is your goal – and I assume that is why you purchased this book – you should base your workouts on basic exercises that cause the greatest metabolic demand, thus causing the desired hormonal response. This is where the concept of "growth centers of the body" comes into play. Only when you use a significant amount of muscle mass during an exercise do you cause the body's endocrine glands to release the needed hormones into the bloodstream. You should spend most of your time working the large muscle groups (i.e. legs, back, chest) with compound movements such as squats, bench presses and bent rows, and less time on smaller bodyparts and isolation exercises. The muscles of the legs, back and chest are truly the growth centers of the body. They contain the greatest amount of muscle

mass, have the ability to carry the most muscle, and look the most impressive when developed. This might sound like common sense to some, but one often sees people spending far more time and energy on their arms than they do on their legs or back. You probably have a few of these people in your gym. (Egad, I hope you are not one of them!)

From this information it would seem that the muscles of the legs, back and chest are best worked with a combination of heavy weights, low to moderate reps and long rest periods, with moderate to high reps, basic movements and short rest periods. That is, of course, assuming you are interested in growing muscle tissue. You could use this rep/weight/rest combination in the same workout or split it up into alternating weeks or months.

In general, testosterone is extremely hard to raise significantly on a consistent basis, but this can be accomplished to some degree if you are willing to work hard enough (and smart enough). Growth hormone on the other hand is easier to affect, but is particularly reliant on proper training/dietary/rest variables. Finally, insulin is very easy to raise, but increase of insulin is desirable only at certain times (i.e. immediately following a workout) and is most dependent on dietary intake of key micro- and macronutrients. Insulin is an extremely anabolic hormone, but it can also make you fat as a house, so don't think eating sweets all day to raise insulin will help you add muscle. It will only make you add blubber.

Up to now we have discussed only anabolic hormones. It is important at this juncture to talk about catabolic hormones (such as cortisol) that break down muscle tissue and how to avoid raising them. Keeping catabolic hormones low through training, diet and supplementation is an exciting new area of research known as "anti-catabolism" which is all the rage (and rightly so) with many magazines, supplement makers and trainers in the know. All we need to say here is that high cortisol levels make you fat, prevent protein synthesis, suppress your immune system and waste hard-earned muscle tissue. Avoid it at all costs! High cortisol levels are caused by overtraining, stress, illness, and to a smaller degree, certain dietary influences. Your workout should never last longer than an hour. After an hour of intense weight training there is a sharp decline in circulating anabolic hormones. Never work out more than two days in a row. Avoid stress and stressful situations (i.e. boneheads, negative people and morons). Besides high cortisol levels there are other ways the body can get into a catabolic state.

Diet

Protein quality and quantity are absolutely essential for growing muscle. There are several ways of assessing protein quality. The most common, and least useful, is the Protein Efficiency Ratio (PER). The PER is an outdated measurement of protein quality that does not reflect human needs. It is based on growth measurements of young rats. Biological Value (BV) is a far more accurate measurement of protein quality. BV represents the

amount of nitrogen (absolutely essential for growth) which can be replaced by one hundred grams of protein in the diet. High-BV proteins cause the greatest nitrogen retention. High-BV proteins also have the greatest effect on insulin-like growth-factor (IGF-I) levels. IGF-I is the growth factor that is released during the destruction of growth hormone (GH) in the liver and is what actually causes most of the growth associated with GH. (2) The amount of growth you can stimulate from GH is directly related to the amount of IGF you can produce. This is why people who have high GH levels but low IGF levels don't grow an ounce of muscle.

IGF is also intimately connected to insulin and has many functions that are similar to insulin (hence the name), but that's another

Gerard Dente

Debbie Muggli

acids (BCAAs), which are the amino acids that are primarily used (oxidized) during exercise, and are anticatabolic in nature. Contrary to what some misinformed nutritionists, vegetarians and supplement manufacturers might try to have you believe, vegetable proteins (including soy) have a low BV score and are very poor for nitrogen retention and IGF stimulation. Vegetable protein might be fine for couch potatoes (a type of vegetable!), but is wholly inferior for growing muscle – the main concern of the bodybuilder.

There has been much debate over which protein is the best for growth. Egg protein is still pushed hard by many manufacturers as the reference protein when they try to sell you egg powder for your protein drink. It is true that eggs have a high BV rating (though whey is still higher), but you must realize that all measurements of protein quality in eggs are based on the whole egg and not the egg white that is used by supplement manufacturers. Also, the heating of the egg white, which is necessary to kill any dangerous organisms (such as salmonella), further degrades the quality of the egg protein. Whole eggs cooked just enough to kill the salmonella are a great source of protein for bodybuilders (along with red meat, turkey, fish, etc.,) but when it comes to getting additional protein from a powdered source, whey is the only way (no pun intended) to go. For an in-depth discussion of whey protein and all of its many benefits, see chapter 5. The BV of egg white (BV = 88) is not much better than that of soy protein (BV = 74), which in my view is real crap. Yeah, I know what you're thinking, 'Hey Will, why don't you tell us what you really think?' I recommend at least 1.0-1.5 grams of protein per pound of bodyweight, of which 30 to 50 percent or more should come from ion-exchange (preferably hydrolyzed) whey protein. You should spread your intake over five or six meals (every three hours), with the largest serving of whey protein immediately following your workout. People who know me and my writing know I don't mind plugging a great product when I see one, and Next Nutrition Designer Whey Protein is probably the best on the market, though there are other whey-protein products that are perfectly fine to use.

extremely complicated story. There are other growth factors associated to high-BV proteins, but nitrogen retention and IGF levels are probably the two most important to muscle growth. Animal and human studies have shown that IGF levels rise in direct proportion to the quality and quantity of protein in the diet. (3) An adequate calorie diet is important for growth, but the quantity and quality of protein in the diet are far more important to the anabolic drive than total calories consumed. (4) (5) The highest-rated BV protein known to man is ion-exchange hydrolyzed whey protein, with ion-exchange nonhydrolyzed whey protein a close second. Whey protein concentrates also contain the highest concentration of branched-chain amino

Carbohydrates are intimately connected

to the anabolic drive, especially when eaten at correct times and in correct amounts. Insulin is directly involved with GH and IGF-I metabolism. Besides just giving us energy for killer workouts, carbs play a host of important biological roles in growth, probably most important of which is the relationship to insulin levels. Insulin management is another exciting new area of research that will have great influences on bodybuilding in the near future. There is a great deal yet to learn, but new discoveries showing how to use insulin for anabolic purposes, and how it works, are being made all the time. Insulin controlled correctly is very anabolic. Indiscriminate carb-eating, which dramatically raises insulin, will just make you fat. Bodybuilders who experiment with injections of insulin without extremely close medical supervision are genuinely asking for trouble in the form of a coma and a host of other potential problems.

Most bodybuilders have probably heard of the glycemic index. Carbohydrates are classified as simple or complex according to their chemical structure, yet this classification does not always reflect how the body will react to them. The glycemic index was designed to indicate the absorption rate of carbohydrates into the bloodstream, and thus their effect on insulin. Low-glycemic foods are absorbed slowly so they do not cause a large insulin spike. High-glycemic foods are absorbed quickly and therefore cause a large influx of insulin to lower the blood sugar. Interestingly enough, many foods we think of as complex cause a quick rise in blood sugar, and some foods we think of as simple sugars do not. For the bodybuilder this means eating low-glycemic carbs throughout the day gives a steady flow of blood sugar and consequently a steady but low flow of insulin, which is essential for its anabolic activity. Going for long periods without eating, or eating too many high-glycemic carbs, causes large fluctu-

Mike Matarazzo

ations of blood sugar followed by equally large insulin spikes with the result of more glucose being converted to bodyfat. This sequence generally leaves the person feeling tired and looking pudgy. Excess carbohydrate of any type, ingested through continuous overfeeding, is easily stored as – you guessed it – fat. I have included a partial listing of glycemic values for some of the more common foods.

There are some disadvantages and drawbacks to the glycemic index that people should be aware of. One major problem is that, although the index tells of the absorption rate of a certain food, it does not tell you why it has that characteristic. For example, ice cream is low on the glycemic index. Why? The fat contained in the ice cream slows down the absorption of the sugar and therefore lowers the glycemic rating of ice cream. Does this mean we should eat ice cream all day long? Obviously not. What this tells us is that there are foods on the glycemic index that are rated low but are still not necessarily good to eat.

Mixing a carb with other foods, fiber, fat and several other factors (such as cooking time) can change its glycemic rating. A classic example of people's confusion concerning the index pertains to fructose. Since fructose is very low on the index, many people think they can eat all the fructose they want. It was also a great marketing scam for food manufacturers. Fructose bypasses a key regulatory point in the utilization of carbohydrates in the glycolytic pathway – the pathway by which glucose is degraded into smaller and smaller units. Suffice it to say, without going into a long biochemical explanation, that fructose readily converts to bodyfat, although it is low on the index. That does not mean a piece or two of fruit a day is going to make you a fat pig, but eating large amounts of fruit or foods high in fructose will definitely hinder the process of fat loss.

Bodybuilders with slow metabolisms should eat 1.0-1.5 grams per pound of bodyweight of low-glycemic carbs spread over five or six meals along with their protein, vegetables, etc. Bodybuilders with fast metabolisms should eat 1.5-2.5 grams per pound of bodyweight. Most bodybuilders overindulge in carbohydrates. Muscle cells will accept only so much insulin-driven glucose and amino acids into the cell, at which point they will shut off, and any additional glucose will be stored as – you guessed it again – fat, or burned as energy. People have different abilities to store glucose in either muscle cells or fat cells.

There is one final and important catch to the insulin-management scheme. After a serious workout the body will shunt blood glucose, which was used for energy during the workout, into muscle and liver cells to replace glycogen stores lost during exercise. This is the time to eat high-glycemic carbohydrates, prefer-

Partial List of Glycemic Index

(Source: Jenkins et al., *American Journal Of Clinical Nutrition*, 1981)

Grains and grain products:

White bread	69
Whole-meal bread	72
Whole-wheat bread	64
Millet	71
Brown rice	66
White rice	72
Whole-wheat spaghetti	40
Corn	59
All-bran cereal	51
Cornflakes	80
Porridge oats	49
Shredded wheat	67
White-flour pancakes	66

Beans/Vegetables:

Carrots	92
White potatoes	70
Sweet potatoes	48
Yams	51
Lentils	29
Kidney beans	29
Black-eyed peas	33
Chick peas	36
Soy beans	15
Lima beans	36

Fruits:

Apples	39
Bananas	62
Oranges	40
Raisins	64
Grapefruit	26
Grapes	45
Cherries	23
Peaches	29

Sugars:

Glucose	100
Fructose	20
Sucrose	59

Dairy:

Ice cream	36
Whole milk	34
Skim milk	32
Yogurt	36

Other:

Honey	87
Peanuts	13
Sausages	28
Potato chips	51

Kim Chizevsky

ably in liquid form for the quickest possible absorption, to stimulate insulin production. After exercise muscle cells are very receptive to glucose, and not a drop of postworkout carbohydrates will be stored as fat – assuming the workout was intense enough. A carbohydrate drink which has glucose/glucose polymers and a small amount of fructose (such as Twinlab's Ultra Fuel) is a perfect postexercise drink which can dramatically aid in muscle remodeling (growth) and repair.

The uptake and effectiveness of postworkout carbohydrates are greatly improved in the presence of high-BV proteins such as whey, and they should always be included in the postworkout drink. I have bodybuilders drink a

concoction of grape juice (which is loaded with glucose), Ultra Fuel, two teaspoons of Creatine and whey protein concentrate, and boy, does it taste like sh—! Six to eight ounces of grape juice, a half to a whole Ultra Fuel, three scoops of whey protein, and water to taste should do the job nicely. Just don't blame me when your muscles get so full you have to buy new clothes. Immediately following a workout is the best time to take advantage of insulin's anabolic properties, but proper insulin management throughout the day is essential to properly manipulating this powerful hormone to your advantage.

The Other Half of Insulin Management: Insulin Sensitivity

Having just the right amount of glucose floating around for a low but continuous supply of insulin is all well and good, but if the insulin cannot get the glucose and amino acids into the cell, you will still have great difficulty making muscle or burning bodyfat. When your cells are resistant to insulin you are said to be insulin insensitive. In the extreme case this condition is known as diabetes. I am of the opinion, as are many researchers I speak with, that most people are somewhat insulin resistant. Many of the eating habits of the average American will lead to subclinical (meaning not bad enough to be considered diabetes) insulin resistance. Diets high in saturated fat and low in fiber, diets overly high in sugar and/or complex carbs, and a lack of certain key micronutrients (which pretty much sums up the average American diet) will make you insulin resistant. To top it all off as it relates to bodybuilders and other athletes who use various drugs, steroids and GH have both been found to cause insulin resistance.

There has been much debate whether or not the absence of certain nutrients from the diet (such as chromium) can lead to insulin resistance and ultimately type II adult onset diabetes, but there is little debate that many of these nutrients can improve insulin resistance when added to the diet of diabetics or people who have subclinical insulin resistance. I am sure you could dig up a doctor who has not seen a nutrition textbook in fifty years or an "all you need are the RDAs"-spouting registered dietitian who will dispute what I have written in this section, but the scientific literature is chock-full of studies showing that various nutrients and drugs can dramatically improve insulin sensitivity. I will touch briefly on a few of these nutrients. Most of them have many additional health and performance benefits and are mentioned and recommended elsewhere in the book.

The role of chromium and its importance to insulin metabolism have been well established. The average American diet is a notoriously poor source of chromium, (6) and that exercise increases the need for it. (7) Although no one blows up with muscle from the simple addition of chromium to his diet, there is no doubt (at least in my mind) that this nutrient improves glucose metabolism, lipid metabolism and insulin-binding in those people who are slightly to severely insulin resistant. Many studies have also shown the nutrients vitamin E, magnesium, essential fatty acids, fiber and possibly vitamin C to improve insulin

sensitivity.(8) Because of the immense benefits not related to insulin metabolism that these nutrients have on health, and the substantial amount of research demonstrating their ability to improve glucose metabolism, coupled with the fact that deficiencies in one or all of these nutrients is common, athletes should definitely supplement their diet regularly with them. In addition to a good multivitamin that contains at least 400 mcg of chromium, you should add 800 to 1000 I.U. of vitamin E, three to six grams of buffered vitamin C, and a full-spectrum multimineral supplement.

As luck would have it, or more likely the incredible design of our food that only nature can supply, many of the foods low on the glycemic index also happen to be high in fiber, which has been shown to improve insulin sensitivity. Yams, brown rice, porridge oats, most varieties of beans, and some other vegetables are low on the index, high on the fiber content, and full of vitamins and minerals. Many foods that are low on the index – e.g. pasta, white rice, ice cream – are so heavily processed as to be basically devoid of vitamins, minerals and fiber and should not be eaten too often. In my view fortifying a food with a few vitamins does not make up for the loss of those same vitamins

Milos Sarcev, Mike Matarazzo and Mauro Sarni.

Dennis
Newman

or the fiber, minerals and vitamins they do not replace.

Although saturated fat can cause insulin resistance, the essential fatty acids (especially the omega-3 fatty acids) improve insulin sensitivity. (9) Not only do they improve insulin sensitivity, but omega-3 fatty acids also have anti-inflammatory, antilipogenic (stops fat storage), cholesterol-lowering, growth-hormone-releasing and anticatabolic properties! (10) What else could you possibly ask for in a nutrient? I go into much more detail about these incredible fatty acids in the next chapter.

Three other supplements that I have

Additional and Optional Nutrients

not covered are optional to the diet. If you want to spend the money, they are definitely worth taking and will really add bang for the buck to your training and nutritional regimen. Creatine monohydrate, vanadyl sulphate and a digestive enzyme complex are the three additional supplements I would recommend. These three supplements, along with the other products mentioned in this chapter and throughout this book, are always part of the off-season and precontest regimen of the bodybuilders and other athletes I work with. Without going into a long explanation, here is a down and dirty guide as to how you should take these additional nutrients.

Add two or three digestive enzyme caps with each meal, a heaping teaspoon or two of creatine to the postworkout drink (after the loading phase that is explained on the label), and 10 to 20 milligrams of vanadyl sulphate to each meal. Adding the enzymes to the diet will help with digestion and assimilation of your nutrients (always desirable), and the creatine and vanadyl are the next best thing to steroids. If I had only enough money to buy either the creatine or the vanadyl, I would definitely choose the creatine.

Conclusion

There are other important points to these anabolic strategies that just cannot be covered here, but I assure you, if you put this information to good use (genetics willing) you could notice significant muscle growth. Of all the chapters in this book, this one and the next on fats have the most relevant and useful information for obtaining your goal of adding new muscle. The nutritional status of many micro- and macronutrients is essential for all of this to work for you. For example, a small deficiency in potassium can stop muscular growth in its tracks. A small deficiency in many nutrients can kill the anabolic drive. Coaxing your body into renewed growth takes some planning and careful manipulation of many variables. For legal, moral and financial reasons the days of just

taking lots of drugs, training heavy and eating everything in sight are gone. The age of making the most of your genetics through other means (e.g. using the information presented in this chapter) is here to stay. Don't let anyone with outdated and incorrect information convince you that you get all the nutrients you need from your food to grow maximum muscle mass or reach your true athletic potential because that's nonsense.

Ronnie Coleman

References

(1) Kraemer, W.J., Physiologic responses to heavy resistance training with short rest periods. *Int. Journal of Sports Medicine.* 8: 247-252, 1987.
(2) Daughaday, W.H., *Endocrine control of growth.* NY, Elsevier. North Holland Press, 1981.
(3) Yahya, Z., et al., Dietary and hormonal influences on plasma insulin like growth factor levels in the rat. *J. Endrocrinology,* 1987; Supple: 71.
(4) Jepson M.M., Bates P.C., Milliard D.J., The role of insulin and thyroid hormones in the regulation of muscle growth and protein turnover in response to dietary protein. *British J. Nutrition.* 5/1988, 59, 397 - 415.
(5) Isley W.L., Underwood L.E., Clemmons D.R., Dietary componenets that regulate serum somatomedin C (IGF-1) in humans. *J Clin Invest,* 1983; 36: 533-537.
(6) Anderson R.A., Koslovsky A.S., Chromium intake, absorption and excretion of subjects consuming self-selected diets. *Am J Clin Nutr,* 41:177-183, 1985.
(7) Anderson R.A., et al. Effect of exercise on serum glucose, insulin, glucagon and chromium excretion. *Diabetes Mar,* 31: 212-6 Vol. 3 1994.
(8) McCarty M.F., Protective benefits of nutritional insurance supplementation in diabetes – an update. *J Opt Nutr,* 2:84-95 Vol. 3 1994.
(9) Liu S., et al Dietary omega-3 and polyunsaturated fatty acids modify fatty acyl composition and insulin binding in skeletal muscle sarcolemma. *Biochem. J.* 299:831-7, 1994.
(10) DiPasquale M.G., Omega-3 Fatty Acids. *Drugs in Sports,* 1:4-6, Vol. 3 1995.

Chapter Four
Who's Afraid of Fat?

Fat. The very word sends a shiver through the biceps of the leanest bodybuilder. Sure, most bodybuilders know there are large differences in the quality of proteins and carbohydrates that we eat, but fat is fat, right? Wrong! The fact is, fats and oils have just as many chemical differences, and thus effects on the body, as do carbohydrates and protein. I know, I know, just when you were getting used to this whole glycemic-index-for-carbs bit, and the biological-value-rating thing for proteins, I come along and throw in a new mind-bender on fats. I apologize for the interruption in your contentedness, but it will be well worth your while to see fat in a new light if building muscle is your goal.

Unfortunately for the much maligned lipid, fats and oils have been lumped together in the minds of most bodybuilders as having the same properties, with the result of bodybuilders trying to avoid all fats and oils for fear of adding bodyfat and looking like the Pillsbury dough boy. Well, I am here to tell you that fats have gotten a bad rap in bodybuilding. There are some good fats, and there are some bad fats. The difference between the two is substantial and of great importance to musclehea... er, I mean us bodybuilders. (Yeah, I know, it's not "PC" to say musclehead any more.) But seriously, to understand the differences among the various types of fats, we have to look at exactly what a fat is. This is where we get into the chemistry of fat,

David Dearth, Lee Priest and Flavio Baccianini

with the good stuff coming later, so bear with me.

Fats and oils are made up of carbon and hydrogen atoms linked together in a chain. On one end you have a methyl group (CH3-), in the middle are carbon atoms linked together making the chain, and on the other end you have a carboxyl group (-COOH). So far, so good.

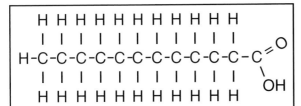

How long the carbon chain is, how many double bonds it has (unsaturated), or no double bonds (saturated), what is attached at the end of the fatty-acid chain (i.e. phosphate group, glycerol, etc.), whether it has been heated and/or chemically processed, what shape the chain takes, and many other variables decide its chemical properties. The different chemical properties of the various potential combinations can make a fat or oil desirable for health, performance and building muscle, or something to be avoided like the plague. As with everything in bodybuilding — supplements, drugs, equipment, etc. — there is also a wide range of differences in fats and oils that should be explored and understood by bodybuilders, or "normal" people for that matter, interested in improving their health and furthering development. Obviously it would be impossible to fully explain the function and nature of every type of fat, but we can look at some of the more important types and their functions, both positive and negative, and make the appropriate recommendations.

Essential Fatty Acids (EFAs)

As with "essential" nutrients (i.e. vitamins, minerals, etc.) or "essential" amino acids, EFAs must be supplied through your diet because the human body cannot make its own. The two essential fatty acids are linoleic acid (LA), which is an omega-6 fatty acid, and alpha-linolenic acid (LNA), which is an omega-3 fatty

Kim Chizevsky

acid. From these two fatty acids the human body can make — through various enzymes — many different types of fatty acids it needs for countless biological functions that maintain and/or improve health and performance. Both LA and LNA are unsaturated fatty acids, which means they have missing hydrogen atoms at certain points in the chain, making double bonds between the carbon atoms. The double bonds between carbon atoms are what make unsaturated oils biologically active, unlike saturated fatty acids which are generally inert.

John Sherman, Andreas Munzer and Porter Cottrell display true sportsmanship!

crease BMR, lower cholesterol/raise HDL, reduce fat storage (antilipogenic), and improve insulin sensitivity, to name only a few functions EFAs have that should interest the bodybuilder.

Several studies have shown animals fed EFAs, combined with a diet that normally causes diabetes in these animals, did not develop diabetes, demonstrating how important these fatty acids are for glucose metabolism. Of paramount importance to bodybuilders, the omega-3 fatty acids in particular have been found to have strong anticatabolic properties through their ability to mediate inflammation, suppress cortisol production, and possibly release growth hormone. Other important functions of EFAs include energy production, control of inflammatory conditions, oxygen transfer, hemoglobin production, cell membrane and organelle integrity, and prostaglandin production.

Prostaglandins (PGEs) are short-lived hormone-like substances that regulate cellular activity on a moment-to-moment basis. They are created from highly unsaturated EFAs by enzyme-controlled oxidation. There are many different types of prostaglandins, which have been categorized by their function and activity. They have been put into three separate groups, or families, which are called PGE-I, PGE-2 and PGE-3.

Prostaglandins are directly involved in regulation of blood pressure, inflammatory responses, insulin sensitivity, immune responses, anabolic/catabolic processes, and hundreds of other functions both known and yet unknown. Obviously a problem with prostaglandin production, or an imbalance in the different types of prostaglandins, would cause all sorts of trouble, and it does.

Most bodybuilders are probably more aware of prostaglandins than they think. For example, the aspirin that is recommended with the ephedra/caffeine stack for fat-burning is used because aspirin blocks the prostaglandin

The human body can make unsaturated fatty acids from saturated fatty acids (by desaturase enzymes), which have no double bonds because they are fully "saturated" with hydrogen atoms. However, the human body is unable to "desaturate" ingested fatty acids at certain points in the chain (third and sixth carbon), and therefore these particular fatty acids (LNA and LA) must be supplied by the diet. Moreover, the body's ability to turn saturated fatty acids into unsaturated fatty acids is limited.

Unfortunately few people get enough EFAs, especially the omega-3 fatty acid LNA, in their diet. Also, EFAs are very reactive to light, heat and oxygen, and go rancid quickly. (This topic will be discussed further when we get to the subject of commercial oils.) Among the many physiological effects EFAs have on the body, EFAs – most notably LNA and other omega-3 fatty acids such as DHA and EPA – increase fatty-acid oxidation (fat burning!), in-that would otherwise reduce the thermogenic (fat-burning) effect of the ephedra/caffeine stack. Most bodybuilders also instinctively know beef is good for building muscle. There is a substance in the fat found in beef, known as conjugated linoleic acid, which blocks the effects of prostaglandin PGE-2, a potentially catabolic prostaglandin, and probably explains bodybuilders' affinity for red meat. Finally, many bodybuilders have found evening primrose oil useful for the liver toxicity caused by oral steroids, especially 17a-alkylated ones such as Anadrol. The substance in evening primrose oil which helps with liver toxicity is gamma-linolenic acid. Gamma-linolenic acid (GLA) is the precursor to the prostaglandin PGE-I, which has strong anti-inflammatory properties. The GLA also replaces the lost essential fatty acids depleted from the liver by oral anabolic steroids. The body converts LA (an omega-6 fatty acid) to GLA under normal circumstances, but this conversion can be partially blocked for various reasons. This is why so many people derive benefits from taking GLA directly.

The effects of EFA deficiency include high blood pressure, sticky platelets, tissue inflammation and related diseases, edema, dry skin and many more. Opinions vary regarding how widespread EFA deficiency is, but essential fatty acids are required in adequate amounts in your diet or serious metabolic disturbances occur – hence the description "essential." Death can occur in severe cases, which are admittedly rare. Regardless, EFAs are needed for burning fat efficiently. Furthermore, there does not have to be a deficiency to obtain benefits from adding EFAs to your diet, just as you do not have to have scurvy to get benefits from taking extra vitamin C. I guess I could have summed up this entire section by writing just those last two sentences, but I knew you would have been disappointed!

Commercial Oils: The Good, The Bad and The Ugly.

The average vegetable oils on the supermarket shelf have been so processed as to be nutritionally useless, or worse, harmful. They are the nutritional oil equivalent of white bread and refined sugar. They are stripped of their naturally occurring antioxidants, phospholipids, EFAs, and other nutritionally important factors required for their own metabolism. The more "unsaturated" an oil is, the more chemically reactive it is – that is, more reactive to heat, light and oxygen and it goes "bad" quickly. Oil manufacturers process the oils to extend shelf life or change their properties for uses in certain foods. Unfortunately the process of extending

Andreas Munzer congratulates a victorious Porter Cottrell.

A true monster of muscle — Paul DeMayo.

polymers and molecular fragments are created. The most thoroughly studied of these byproducts are trans-fatty acids. Many researchers have concluded that trans-fatty acids play a causative role in cancer and other degenerative diseases.

Dr. Marry Enig, a researcher who has studied extensively the subject of trans-fatty acids, which are found in refined vegetable oils, shortenings and margarines, has concluded that trans-fatty acids raise cholesterol and lower HDL, interfere with proper immune response, decrease test-osterone in animals, decrease insulin response, and alter liver enzyme activity. Ouch! Definitely not what the bodybuilder needs for growing muscle and maintaining health. Recent news reports have stated that margarine has been found to be worse for you than butter. It is the trans-fatty acids that are responsible for this finding, so pass on the veggie-oil spread the next time you need something to put on your toast.

Just as the shape a fatty acid takes is essential to its function, very specific enzymes and membrane structures fit very specific fatty acids, which carry out various functions in the body. Though trans-fatty acids have the same number of carbon and hydrogen atoms as the fatty acid they once were (known as a cis-fatty acid), their shape has been radically altered. The change in shape from "cis" to "trans" competes for enzymes, blocking the action of the cis-fatty acid, but is unable to carry out the biological role of the cis-fatty acid. With few exceptions cis-fatty acids are what occur naturally. Trans-fatty acids are man-made, and the body has no way to adequately deal with the chemically altered fat, which causes the wide range of problems mentioned previously. Besides their shape there are many other reasons why these altered fats appear to play havoc with the system. The percentage of trans-fatty acids, not to mention the other by-products we have not even touched upon, in a given product depends on the amount and type of processing. On average vegetable-oil products that are hard at room temperature

shelf life does nothing to extend human life! The average vegetable oil has been solvent extracted and/or extracted under high temperatures (partially hydrogenated), bleached, deodorized and generally trashed. During these processes toxic byproducts such as trans-fatty acids, cross-linked fatty-acid chains, dimers,

(e.g. margarine and shortenings) tend to contain more toxic byproducts such as trans-fatty acids than do products that are liquid at room temperature (e.g., vegetable oil).

In general all the supermarket oils, such as corn, canola and soybean, have been partially hydrogenated (heated) and/or heavily processed. The only exception is extra virgin olive oil, which by the definition of "extra virgin" must be unprocessed. However, olive oil is predominantly a mono-unsaturated oil (has only one double bond) and contains inadequate amounts of EFAs. Differing amounts of EFAs are found in our foods, but processing has lowered the amounts substantially. If you want to add some much-needed EFAs to your diet, one to three tablespoons of flax-seed oil in a protein drink or salad is highly recommended for health, performance and potential muscle-building benefits.

Linoleic acid (LA) deficiency is much rarer than alpha-linolenic (LNA) deficiencies. This variance has the result of causing an imbalance between the two essential fatty acids, which leads to further negative metabolic effects, or "omega-6 poisoning" as was explained to me by Dr. Udo Erasmus, the author of *Fats that Heal/Fats that Kill*. LNA and other omega-3 oils and their derivatives appear to be responsible for the majority of health and performance benefits. Flax oil is the highest known source of the omega-3 fatty acids LNA (45-65%), with the remainder being LA (15%), mono-unsaturated fatty acids, and a small amount of saturated fatty acids. The flax oil must be completely unprocessed and kept from light, heat and air.

You can find flax oil in the refrigerated section of any good health-food store. Unprocessed high-quality oils are like milk, eggs and meat in that they spoil quickly (go rancid) if not refrigerated constantly and eaten shortly after opening. Dr. Erasmus, who is probably the world authority on oils both good and bad for health, recommends consuming flax oil or any fresh unprocessed oil within three to six weeks of opening the bottle if it is kept in the fridge. I am sure now you can see why the commercial oil companies process oils to such extremes. As a side note, Dr. Erasmus feels that using flax oil exclusively as a source of EFAs is fine for short periods of up to six months, but for long-term use a more balanced oil which has LNA and LA in a 2:1 ratio (flax oil has a 4:1 ratio) is best for health and performance in the long run. Such an oil is produced by the Flora company (800-446-2110 if you're interested) or can be made by mixing two parts flax oil to one part unprocessed safflower oil. My personal strategy with many of

The beautiful Anja Schreiner

Eddie Robinson

Oil Controversy

You should be aware that most of the research on the omega-3 fatty acids has been done on the fish oils eicosapentaenoic acid (EPA) and docosahexaenoic acid (DHA), which was mentioned only briefly. These two fatty acids can be made in the human body from LNA, which is found in flax oil and other sources. There has been some debate that people might not be able to make this conversion of LNA to EPA and DHA and thus will not be able to obtain the benefits of EPA and DHA and should just eat the fish oils. I do not generally agree with this position. The benefits of flax oil have been demonstrated repeatedly in the research, and anecdotal evidence of researchers has continued to be positive. Unless a person has some serious metabolic problems, the pathway for the conversion of LNA to the highly unsaturated EPA and DHA will eventually establish itself given a short adjustment time. The number of people who genuinely cannot make this conversion has been estimated to be less than two percent of the population.

Although LNA can be made into EPA and DHA, the reverse cannot take place. There are other benefits that are obtained from LNA, that is separate from the other two fatty acids (EPA and DHA). Finally, in a perfect world where both oils (LNA from flax oil and the fish oils EPA and DHA) were produced under similar processes, the argument of which oil to take would be more relevant. Flax oil is produced under low temperatures devoid of light and oxygen – conditions which are absolutely essential for its properties and to avoid rancidity. Though the fish oils are far more reactive than LNA (because they are more unsaturated) and spoil easily, EPA and DHA are squeezed out of fish parts and are not protected from light, heat and oxygen. This means they are often quite rancid. To get your fish oils, eat fresh fish. To get the benefits of the essential fatty acids I have mentioned throughout this chapter, take the flax oil.

the bodybuilders and other athletes I train is to use flax oil during the precontest phase of a diet and the more balanced oil (made by Flora) during the off-season.

Back To Bodybuilding

Gerard Dente

OK, if you survived that long and dry talk on the chemistry of fats, let's get back to the subject of bodybuilding. The reader should understand clearly that there are certain fats and oils to avoid, and there are fats and oils that should be added to the diet. As a trainer for many precontest and off-season bodybuilders, I have never given in to the high-carb, low-fat diet because I just don't think it works very well for bodybuilders – maybe for couch potatoes, but not for bodybuilders. I have seen far better results with a diet of moderate to high protein, moderate amounts of high-quality fat, and low to moderate carbs. The ratio of these nutrients can change depending on many variables such as off-season, precontest, age or sex. The ever controversial and always ingenious "guru" Dan Duchaine put it best: "For the athlete consider reverting your modern diet to one of higher dietary fat. Rearranging it so that you consume 30 percent dietary fat calories may be magical." (*Muscle Media 2000*, October-November '94, p. 36). I completely agree with his assessment.

I have known and/or trained several bodybuilders who have won national-level titles eating low carbs and fats from red meat and flax oil right up to the day of the show. Of course, they don't spread this information around as they don't want you to know their secret. They achieved a condition they had never been able to obtain using the traditional low-fat, high-carb diet, and when they tried a low-carb, low-fat approach, they were so tired they could hardly walk much less train intensely. Sound familiar?

Recently a friend and client of mine, who is a medical doctor and avid weight trainer, was having trouble losing weight. He just couldn't get that last 10 pounds off. He trained with weights, did his aerobics and ate a high-protein, high-carb, low-fat diet. I told him to add two to three tablespoons of flax oil to his diet. Not surprisingly, he resisted my advice to actually add fat to his diet to lose weight. After I worked on him for a month or so, he gave it a try. Two months after adding in the flax oil, he had lost 12 pounds of fat, gained four pounds of muscle, and his cholesterol had gone down 50 points! He said to me, "If anyone had told me in medical school that I could add 42 grams of fat a day (14 grams of fat per tablespoon times 3) to my diet and lose fat and gain muscle, I would have told him he was crazy. "

As a rule, EFAs from flax oil, nuts, seeds, deep-water fish and unprocessed vegetable oils should be a third of your fat calories regardless of what percent from fat your diet contains. The other two-thirds can come from high-quality nonprocessed lean meats and other sources such as top round, fish, chicken, the occasional greasy burger, eggs, low-fat cottage cheese and small amounts of butter and olive oil. Avoid any type of luncheon meats as they contain bad fats, bad protein, bad chemicals

The incredible Michael Francois

and sugar! Fats to avoid are processed commercial vegetable oils, margarine, shortenings, any kind of hydrogenated oil products (which are jammed into virtually everything), any type of fried food, and old rancid oils of any kind. These fats impair health, immunity, performance and ultimately longevity. Always make sure to take adequate amounts of vitamins and minerals (see chapter 3) because they are essential for the body to assimilate and metabolize fat, protein and carbohydrates. Keep your intake of antioxidants high for strong immunity, free-radical protection, and the many other benefits mentioned elsewhere in this book.

A final word of warning: Raising your fat intake without lowering your carb intake will usually result in serious fat deposition. Moderate-fat and high-carb diets are a definite no-no if you want to continue to be able to tie your own shoelaces. The right type of fats, in the correct amounts, actually causes the human body to release fatty-acid stores, but not in the presence of high glucose levels — and glucose is primarily derived from carbohydrates. High blood glucose levels blunt the fat-burning effect and impair the body's ability to metabolize fats, which usually end up on your butt!

Bibliography

Lehninger,A., Nelson, D., Cox, M. *Principles of Biochemistry,* Second Edition, Worth Publishers, NY, NY, 1993.

(*)Erasmus, U. *Fats that Heal/Fats that Kill,* Alive Books, Burnaby, BC, Canada, 1993.

Dray F., et al. Role of prostaglandins on growth hormone secretion: PGE-l a physiological stimulator. *Advances in Prostaglandin and Thromboxane Research.* 8:1321-8, 1980.

Clouatre, D. *Anti-Fat Nutrients,* Pax Publishing, San Francisco, CA, 1993.

Brisson, G. *Lipids in Human Nutrition,* Burgess, Inglewood, NY, 1981.

Holman, T. Essential Fatty Acids and Prostaglandins. *Progress in Lipid Research,* Vol. 20, Pergamon Press, Elmsford, NY, 1981.

Needlemen P., et al. Triene prostaglandins; prostaglandin and thromboxane biosynthesis and unique biologic properties. *Proc. Nat Acad Sci* 76:944-48, 1979.

Colgan, M. *Optimum Sports Nutrition,* Advanced Research Press, Ronkonkoma, NY, 1993.

DiPasquale M.G. Omega-3 fatty acids. *Drugs in Sports* 1:4 6 Vol. 3, 1995.

(*)= *Fats that Heal/Fats that Kill* is probably the most complete and comprehensive book on the subject of fats and oils for health and performance. It is highly recommended reading for anyone interested in the subject.

**Mr. Olympia
Dorian Yates
captures another
title!**

Chapter Five
Whey Protein Concentrate
The Life Extension Protein

Australia's Lee Priest

A great deal of research has been occurring regarding the value of micronutrients and other compounds for the purpose of preventing disease and extending human life. Recently, however, researchers have been taking a closer look at some of the macronutrients (most notably certain types of proteins) and their ability to improve immunity, prevent disease and possibly extend life. We have long known that different types of proteins can have profound effects on the metabolism of humans and animals. Researchers have lately been turning their attention to one protein in particular. This protein is called whey protein concentrate (WPC). WPC appears to have properties that are unique in their ability to improve health and stave off the ravages of aging. Below is a small example of the powers of this extraordinary protein.

WPC Raises Glutathione

Glutathione is arguably the most important water-soluble antioxidant found in the body. It is a naturally occurring sulfur amino-acid tripeptide (composed of L-cysteine, L-glutamic acid and glycine). An age-related decline in glutathione production is correlated with many diseases associated with free-radical damage of organs and various systems. For example, the brains of people with Alzheimer's disease, a condition of accelerated aging, contain lower concentrations of glutathione and increased levels of lipid peroxidation, compared to nondemented elderly, (1) but can have adequate levels of vitamin E. (2) In the brain tissue of people with Parkinson's disease, the severity of cellular deficit can be predicted accurately by the concentration of glutathione, while the levels of ascorbate, an important water-soluble antioxidant, in the brain were virtually no different from controls. (3) These are only two of many examples showing the importance of glutathione in diseases related to free-radical oxidative damage. In short, the ability of a cell to survive an oxidative assault appears to reflect its ability to regenerate its stores of glutathione. (4)

WPC was compared to all known commercially available purified proteins (e.g., casein, spirulina, soy, wheat, corn, scenedesmus, egg albumin, fish, and beef) for their ability to raise glutathione levels to normal values. Mice fed these proteins at 20 g protein per l00 g of feed did not show elevated levels of glutathione above normal, but when WPC was added to their diet, glutathione levels rose above normal values. The mice that were fed pure WPC (20g/l00g feed) showed consistent increases in the levels of glutathione (5) as measured by the concentrations of glutathione found in their spleen, liver and heart. Also, mice fed the WPC diet lived an average of five to six months longer (corresponding to an increase from 55 years to 80 years of age for humans) than the mice fed any other type of protein. (6) Interestingly, when sulfur containing amino acids, which are substrates for glutathione synthetase, were added to the non-WPC protein diets, there was still no rise in glutathione above normal level. These findings have wide-ranging implications for people interested in life extension and the prevention and possible control of many degenerative diseases.

Dr. Gustavo Bounous of the Montreal General Hospital Research Institute and his colleagues have done most of this research. He states, "This discovery could provide a method for efficiently increasing cellular glutathione levels for any purpose for which elevated glutathione levels are desired, such as for drug detoxification, arteriosclerosis, Alzheimer's and Parkinson's diseases; cellular protection against oxygen and its metabolites such as peroxides, free radicals or foreign compounds, carcinogens, irradiation, immunodeficiency states, etc." (*Clin Invest Med* Vol. 14 1991).

Apparently several important factors lead WPC to have these unique properties. First and foremost, the WPC must be at least 90% or more undenatured. When denatured WPC is used, there is no rise in glutathione above normal values. (7) The normally high temperatures that are employed during the processing of whey protein and other proteins destroy the native conformation (the unique shape of the molecule) by destroying di-sulphide bonds of the protein. Di-sulphide bonds are among the intramolecular forces that give the protein its native three-dimensional shape that

Mike Matarazzo

Terry Mitsos

It is very interesting to note that intact glutamyl-cysteine groups with di-sulphide links are extremely rare in edible animal and plant proteins (Bounous, Gold, 1991). In fact, a computer literature search revealed that they are limited only to whey proteins, which have substantial amounts of glu-cys groups, and the ovomucoid fraction of egg whites (8), but only minute amounts can be found in that fraction of the egg protein. It has been theorized that the undenatured (native) conformation of the WPC protects the glutamylcysteine groups and their di-sulphide links from the digestive enzymes of the stomach, and thus the peptides are able to pass through the intestinal mucosa into the bloodstream intact. This would explain the inability of denatured WPC to raise glutathione levels.

is necessary for biological activity. Only WPC that is processed using low-temperature methods such as membrane filtration and ion-exchange filtration appear to survive the process undenatured. Unfortunately most WPC is produced using less expensive higher-temperature methods. The amino-acid profile will "spec" out the same (i.e. will have the same amino-acid sequence), but its biological activity is lost. In addition to its undenatured state the WPC must have a high percentage of glutamylcysteine groups, which are located primarily in the serum albumin, B-lactoglobulin and immunoglobulin fraction of the protein.

WPC Increases Immunity and Fights Cancer

The ability of different proteins to enhance immunity against dimethylhydrazine (DMH)-induced tumors was investigated. DMH is known to be a powerful carcinogen. Again WPC demonstrated its ability to fight degenerative diseases. After 24 weeks of DMH treatment the size and incidence of tumors were substantially less in mice fed WPC than in mice fed all other proteins. (9) WPC was also found to be highly effective against microbial infections such as salmonella and other microbial challenges. (10) WPC appears to be effective at increasing both humoral and cellular immune responses. Mice given an antigenic challenge by injections of sheep red-blood cells exhibited an immune response five times greater than normal when WPC was the source of protein (11), compared to any other type of protein (soy, beef, casein, etc.).

Interestingly enough, every time WPC was mixed with the other proteins in the diets of mice, the immune response was improved above normal, but never as high as when WPC was the only source of protein. It is particularly important to note that the higher immune response to injections of sheep red-blood cells in WPC-fed mice represents a true enhancement of the immune response produced by dietary protein type, and not a shift in the timing of the peak response (Bounous, Kongshavn, Gold, 1988). The ability of WPC to improve immunity against a wide range of challenges is believed to be a result of the rise in glutathione, but other mechanisms are still being investigated.

WPC Raises IGF-1

Insulin-like growth factor (IGF-I) is the growth factor that is released during the destruction of growth hormone (GH) in the liver and is what actually causes the growth associated with GH.(12) Studies have shown IGF-I rises in direct proportion to the quality and quantity of protein in the diet.(13) The quality of a protein is most accurately assessed using the biological value (BV) rating for proteins, as opposed to the outdated protein efficiency ratio (PER). WPC has the highest known BV rating of any protein.(14) Undenatured WPC has a BV rating of 104. Hydrolyzing the WPC, making di-, tri-, and oligopeptides (short and longer chains of amino acids) further increases its BV to 149 - 159, whereas egg white has a BV of only 88. Several recent studies have shown intact peptides to be far superior for IGF stimulation and nitrogen retention than intact whole proteins or free amino acids (Leibovitz 1994). WPC also has the highest known percentage of branched-chain amino acids (BCAAs) of any

protein. These are the amino acids primarily used (oxidized) during exercise, and are anti-catabolic in muscle-wasting states. (15,16)

The importance of this information should be self-evident to anyone concerned about muscle-wasting – athletes, AIDS patients, cancer patients – and people coping with reduced GH levels that occur with age. The exact connection to GH, IGF-1, WPC and aging is unclear at best, but a certain amount of healthy speculation seems warranted considering the findings. Obviously, further research is needed for any definitive answers.

Ronnie Coleman

Conclusion

Believe it or not, there are other positive effects WPC has that are not covered here for lack of space. The type of processing and the quality of the starting material in the different grades of whey protein determine the amount of denaturation and the percent of glutamylcysteine groups of the WPC. This is an essential consideration for its effectiveness. When searching for a commercial product, consider the important properties of whey-protein concentrates, and improved health, performance and resistance to diseases could be the result.

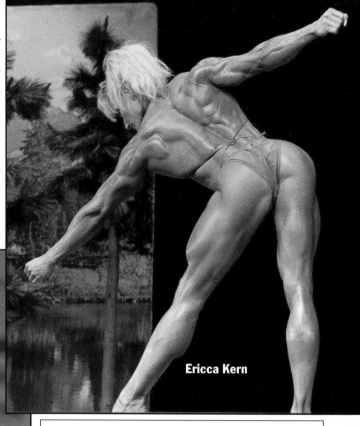

Ericca Kern

Lee Priest

References

(1) Chia, L.S.,Thompson, J.E.,Moscorello, M.A., X-ray diffraction evidence for myelin disorder in brain from humans with Alzheimer's disease. *Canadian Bio-phys acta Ser Biomemb* 775: 308-312, 1984.

(2) Schafer, L.,Thorling, E.B., Lipid peroxidation and antioxidant supplementation in old age. *Scand J Clin Lab Invest* 50: 69-75, 1990.

(3,5,7,8) Bounous, G., Gold, P., The biological activity of undenatured dietary whey proteins: role of glutathione. *Clin Invest Med* Vol. 14:4 296-309, 1991.

(4) Kinsella, J., Lawrence, D., Determination of glutathione in lymphocytes and possible association of redox state and capacity of lymphocytes. *J Biochem.* 198: 571–579,1981.

(6) Bounous, G., Gervais, F.,Amer, V., Batist, G., Gold, P., The influence of dietary whey protein on tissue glutathione and the diseases of aging. *Clin Invest Med* Vol. 12 1989.

(9) Bounous, G., Dietary whey protein inhibits the development of dimethylhydrazine-induced malignancy. *Clin Invest Med* 12: 213-217, 1988.

(10) Sadler, R., The benefits of dietary whey protein concentrate on the immune response and health. *S. Afr. J. Dairy Sci* 24: No. 2, 1992.

(11) Bounous, G,. Kongshavn, P., Gold, P., The immunoenhancing property of dietary whey protein concentrate. *Clin Invest Med* Vol.11: 271-278, 1988.

(12) Daughaday, W.H., *Endocrine control of growth.* NY, Elsevier, North Holland Press. 1981.

(13) Yahya, Z., Dietary and hormonal influences on plasma insulin-like growth factor (IGF) levels in the rat. *J. Endocrinology,* Suppl: 71, 1987.

(14) Renner, E., *Milk and dairy products in human nutrition.* Volkswirtschaftlicher Verlag. Munich Germany, 1983.

(15) May, M.E., Buse, M.G., Effects of branched-chain amino acids on protein turnover. *Diabetes Metab Rev.* 5 (3) : 227-245 1989.

(16) Nair, K.S., et al., Leucine as a regulator of whole body and skeletal muscle protein metabolism in humans. *Am J Physiol.* 263: 928-34 1992.

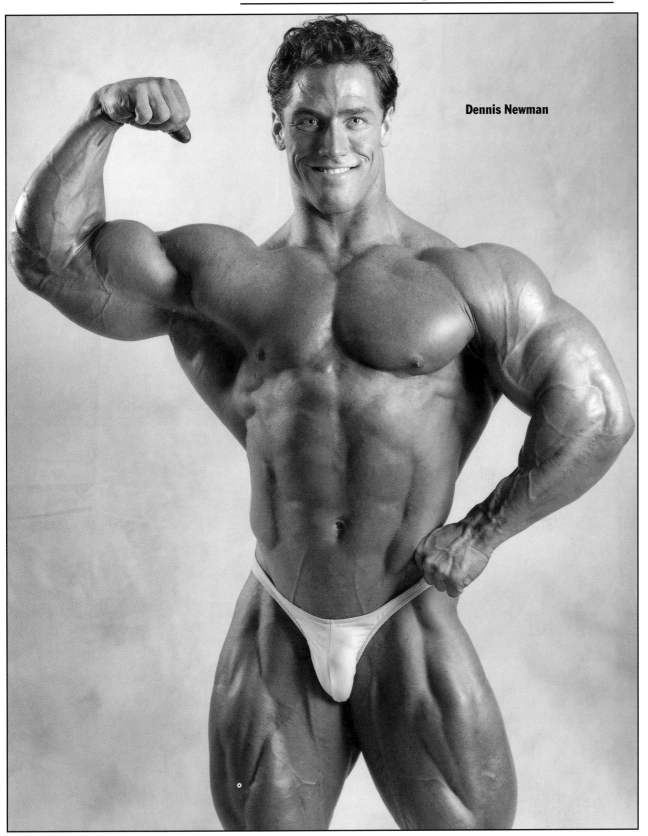

Dennis Newman

Chapter Six
How To Choose A Fat-Burning Supplement

It seems every day a new supplement of some kind comes out on the market. Some are based on solid research, some are based on marketing, and others are based on pseudo-science and sheer lies. The latest rage is fat-burning nutrients. The concept of compounds that burn fat (e.g. inositol, choline) has been around for some time, though none of them did a damn thing for losing fat. They were great for losing weight by emptying your pockets of money! Now, however, new supplements that are utilizing herbs containing ephedrine, caffeine and other compounds (such as aspirin) in specific ratios are demonstrating actual clinically proven results for losing fat. Unfortunately some manufacturers are putting out products

that are questionable as to their effectiveness, safety and quality. Some products contain less than half of what the label claims, or worse yet, none of what the label claims! Along with the makers of quality fat-burning supplements who follow strict quality-control guidelines and read the studies done on these substances, there are the inevitable companies that are out to make a buck by making substandard products whose only effects are to eat up your money and leave you disappointed.

As with all supplements before, many people are left feeling they need to be a rocket scientist to figure out what to buy. Let me give you a quick example. Some time ago a body-builder I train came up to me and said he had

Sharon Bruneau

bought a fat-burning supplement with the ingredients I mentioned as being good for burning fat and giving you energy. The product contained ephedra, caffeine, L-carnitine and chromium picolinate. This seemed to me at first glance to be a decent product, but with further examination I discovered it was not such a good buy after all. It had 200 milligrams of caffeine, 5 milligrams of ephedra, 20 milligrams of L-carnitine and 25 micrograms of chromium picolinate, or so the label claimed. Basically you would get a big blast of caffeine (the cheapest ingredient in the product) without enough of the other ingredients to do a thing for you. The guy had paid 25 bucks to get a caffeine high!

At this point I decided this book should include a chapter on the latest supplements that get rid of adipose tissue – fat, blubber, lard, etc. – and what is needed to make a good product. Believe me, it takes a great deal more than you might think to produce a high-quality, well-designed product which contains some of the ingredients listed above and can be sold for a reasonable price. Most companies will figure out how much it costs to make and how much profit can be made, then figure out how much of the ingredients to put in the product. A good company will decide what should go in first (hopefully based on some kind of research), then decide how much it will cost the consumer.

I knew if I was going to do a proper job of this chapter I would have to speak to a few people who are on top of the research concerning fat-burning products. Curt Hendrix and Dr. Dallas Clouatre were definitely the men for the job. Curt has spent a great deal of time researching herbs, vitamins and other nutrients for the purpose of fat loss, improved health and energy – topics which are definitely on the minds of most bodybuilders. I have spent long hours with Curt on the phone discussing all sorts of supplements pertaining to fat loss and health, and the conversation is always educational and interesting. He is a chemist by training and education, and the chairman of Nature's Best Secrets (soon to be Natural Science Corp. of America). His company makes an herbal-based product with certain amino acids, vitamins and other nutrients that is first rate. I use it, and so do the bodybuilders I train to cut up for a show or stay lean in the off-season.

Included in the conversation was Dr. Dallas Clouatre, author of the book *Anti-Fat Nutrients*, who works with Curt in formulating products. This is a conversation we had on these products and what you should look for in a good supplement of this type.

Dennis Newman

Paul Dillett and Vince Taylor

volume each herb takes up in the capsule and the volume of the inactive portions of the whole herb make it impossible to include any kind of useful dosage of the active ingredient you need to get a real effect. In general, 75 to as much as 400 milligrams or more of the active ingredient is required to produce a noticeable effect on the system.

Will: So where does that leave you?

Curt H: It leaves you having to take a huge number of pills to get a useful dosage of the herb's active ingredient, or just wasting money by not taking enough. If you extract the active ingredients from the herb, you can dramatically increase the strength and concentration of the active ingredients you are looking for while reducing the number of pills you need to take to a realistic number. Unfortunately many companies just sprinkle in small amounts of many whole herbs. This makes for great label decoration, but does not yield the dosage that you need for the results you want.

Will: Why do they do this?

Curt H: Cost. Herbal extracts cost a great deal more than whole herbs, and the

Debbie Muggli

Hey, you can work out for years and never see a cut if the muscle is covered by fat. Drugs are becoming more and more dangerous, and harder to find as a result of stricter laws which are being enforced with ever greater regularity. You would be better off turning to natural alternatives, which we are going to discuss here. They can be more or less effective than some illegal drugs for the same purpose.

Will: I know people have been using herbs for thousands of years in other parts of the world, but they are relatively new to the West. What are some of the problems people face when trying to buy an herbal-based product for fat loss or other purposes?

Curt H: The first thing that is critical to know when buying any herbal product is the difference between a whole herb and an herbal extract. The strongest of naturally occurring herbs might contain 2 percent of an active ingredient — i.e. 98 percent of the herb has no effect at all. That means that, if you have a formula containing many different herbs, the consumer is not trained to know the difference. They only notice the difference when they use a properly made herbal-extract product. The extract can be up to 20 times more powerful than the original herb. If you see 10 or 15 herbs in a product that are not expressed as extracts, and the recommended dosage on the bottle is three or four capsules, that's a pretty good tip it won't do a thing for you, and you will be throwing money away. There are companies making high-quality herbal products, but they are unfortunately in the minority.

Will: I know many people using ephedrine- and caffeine-based products for fat loss and increased energy ultimately become exhausted and wired out, especially when the adrenal glands get overtaxed. What can be done about this?

Dr. C: The most obvious recommendation is to take a day off from the product each week, and two to three weeks off after three months of using ephedra/caffeine-based supplements. When you manufacture such a product, you must take into consideration the strain on the various systems of the body that are affected. Unfortunately the additional ingredients that need to be added to a well-formulated product to counteract some of the demands placed on the body's various systems by these herbs will greatly increase the cost of producing the supplement. Many manufacturers of these products do not address this issue at all, or just sprinkle in inadequate amounts of these important ingredients in order to keep manufacturing costs down.

Will: If cost is not the main concern, what should these additional nutrients do?

Dr. C: A well-designed fat-burning supplement should have ingredients to support the adrenal glands and the thyroid. It should contain the various minerals, such as magnesium, which these products can make the body excrete or use at a greater rate. It should have nutrients that assist in the increased usage of fatty acid and finally it should address the increase in free radicals that are produced with the increase in metabolism. (Note: Free radicals are byproducts of metabolism which are destructive to the body.) Also, a good product should include nutrients that regulate blood sugar and insulin, which is essential for fat loss. You really

have to consider many biochemical processes. You can't just take something to hype your system up, and ignore the stress the body faces with this type of stimulation. It's like shaving the heads down on a V-6 engine to get the compression of a high-output V-8 engine. Sure, it will run faster than before, but how long do you think the motor will last under the strain?

Will: Along with the ephedra/caffeine stack, what are the other nutrients that should be included in the formula, or taken separately, to counteract the negative effects and assist the body's fat-burning ability?

Lee Priest

Dr. C: Without going too deeply into the science, for blood sugar and insulin regulation you need chromium polynicotinate and vanadyl

Tonya Knight

sulphate. For helping the fatty acid to cross the cell wall into the mitochondria, so it can be used as energy and not stored as fat, L-carnitine is essential. Minerals that should be included are magnesium, copper and potassium. For thyroid and adrenal support you need iodine, L-tyrosine and a host of substrates and cofactors such as pantethine, B-6, copper and many others, which must be present in adequate amounts to support these complex reactions. Remember that these nutrients can play many different roles in the body, and are certainly not limited to what has been mentioned here.

Will: What about antioxidant protection from the increase in metabolism and resulting production of free radicals?

Dr. C: Because the liver is responsible for so many functions in the body such as detoxifying poisons, fat metabolism, energy production and countless other processes vital to health, it is important to include antioxidants specific to the liver. Milk thistle seed extract and hawthorn berry extract contain significant amounts of antioxidant flavonoids which support liver function and combat free radicals. We use green tea extract as our source of caffeine instead of cola nut or guarana (the two most common sources of caffeine in most fat-burning products) because it contains 40 percent polyphenols, which are powerful antioxidants and anticancer agents. Additional vitamin C and E are also recommended. (See chapters 3 and 8.) There are several other noteworthy herbs containing large amounts of various antioxidants that can be used.

Will: It seems as though these extracts, along with the additional vitamins, would be very useful for people using anabolic steroids who want to avoid liver damage. What do you think about that?

Curt H: I wouldn't want to speculate specifically on their ability to mitigate the effects of steroids on the liver as I am not aware of any research on it, but I will say that they are generally good for any type of liver stress, and also improve the function of, and protect, a person's liver that is not under stress.

Will: What about adding aspirin to the mix?

Dr. C: Adding aspirin definitely increases the fat-burning potential of the ephedra/caffeine mix. This has been shown clinically. We recommend salix alba, an extract of white willow bark, which is related chemically and pharmacologically to aspirin. It can be taken in addition to aspirin or alone.

Will: How would you compare the ephedrine/caffeine/aspirin stack to Clenbuterol?

Dr. C: The herbal mix and aspirin is as strong a fat-burning formula as you would want or need to take. I can't see any reason to take anything stronger, so there is no real need for a comparison. Besides, Clenbuterol is illegal and the herbal mix is not. (Note: The FDA plans to make all products containing ephedrine and caffeine illegal in the near future because these products are cutting into the pharmaceutical giants' profits from diet drugs. If you care about your rights to be able to purchase such products in the future, you had better write your congress representative telling him or her that you do not want these products taken off the market.)

Will: Good point. Are there different grades of quality in the same herb?

Curt H: Definitely. Let me give you a small example. As I mentioned before, we use green tea as our source of caffeine because of the polyphenols and other compounds that are beneficial to health. You can buy green tea that has 10 percent or less polyphenols, or you can buy green tea that has 60 percent polyphenols. The difference in cost can be 30 to 40 dollars a kilogram. That's a huge cost difference when you are designing a product, so the consumer should look for the highest quality possible when buying an herbal product. The cost and quality difference is true of most herbs besides the green tea.

Will: Is there anything people should know about other supplements they buy for fat-burning such as chromium, L-carnitine and vanadyl sulphate?

Curt H: There are quality differences in virtually all vitamins, minerals, herbs, etc. Obviously it would be impossible to go down the list here. However, there is one very important point that will help. When reading the label of a supplement, you should look for the ingredients to be listed as "elemental values." One of the best examples of this is chromium picolinate.

Chromium picolinate is approximately 12 percent chromium. The rest is made up of the picolinate portion of the compound. If you read "200 micrograms of chromium picolinate per tablet" on the bottle, it could mean you are only getting 24 micro-grams of the mineral chromium (12 percent of 200). If you wanted to get 400 micrograms of elemental chromium, which is really the minimum amount you need, you would have to take a little over 3500 micrograms of chromium picolinate.

Will: Wow! So what you are saying is, if a supplement is to give you 400 micrograms of elemental chromium, you will have to use 3500 micrograms of chromium picolinate to achieve that dosage. If the label expresses the chromium as the elemental value (the amount of actual chromium in the tablet), you know that you are getting the amount of the ingredient you paid for.

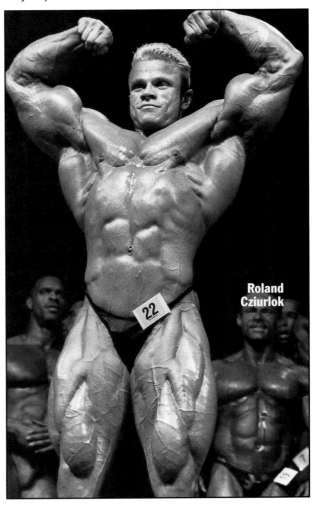

Roland
Cziurlok

Curt H: Exactly. Remember, you don't care about how much picolinate is in the product, only how much elemental chromium there is, and the chromium makes up a very small part of the compound.

Will: What about the other supplements I mentioned?

Curt H: The same holds true for them. L-carnitine is approximately 67 percent carnitine, and the rest is the tartrate part of the compound. They all make up different percentages of a particular nutrient, but you should always look for numbers expressed as elemental values to be sure you are getting the dosage you want.

Will: That is extremely useful information for bodybuilders spending their hard-earned money on supplements. I think readers can put it to good use and in the near future could see cuts in muscles they never knew they had!

Conclusion

Well, there you have it. It should be obvious to the reader that there is more to a well-made fat-burning supplement than just loading it up with caffeine and ephedrine. I have always been hesitant to recommend any type of fat-burning supplement to my clients because there were so many other nutrients they had to buy to make it more effective and less harsh on the system. Obviously you should always look closely at the ingredients listed on any fat-burning product. Are high-quality extracts used? Are there meaningful amounts of the ingredients listed? Are the vitamins and minerals listed as elemental values? Are the ingredients even relevant to the intended product? These are just a few of the questions that must be asked when looking for a decent fat-burning product — or any other product for that matter.

Just because a company posts a long list of ingredients does not mean they are all in the product at a dosage that will do you any good. This is how many companies cheat the buyer out of his money. As P.T. Barnum once said, "No one ever went broke underestimating the intelligence of the American public." He was right. Lots of people are getting rich in the supplement industry by underestimating the intelligence of the public. Don't get scammed. If the company does not list those ingredients the way they should so that you can make an informed decision, call them and ask why not. Don't even bother, unless you don't mind buying that ingredient separately, with a fat-burning product that contains tiny amounts of multiple ingredients. The only company I am aware of that truly attempts to put in virtually all the ingredients a fat-burner should have to be effective long term, healthful, and not burn your body and adrenal glands out is Nature's Best Secrets. To date, their product (called Slim Science) is the only one I will recommend to the athletes and other people I work with. Nature's Best Secrets can be reached at 1-800-936-2378.

Aaron Baker

Milos Sarcev and
Sharon Bruneau

Chapter Seven
Steroids: Then and Now

"Better living through modern chemistry" was the battle cry of many strength athletes from the late '60s to early '80s. T-shirts with a caricature of a Wheaties cereal box that read "Steroids, the breakfast of champions" were a commonplace sight in many gyms around the country. Although bodybuilders and powerlifters took the brunt of the antisteroid "just say no"

political correctness that sprung up around the mid-'80s, steroid use was also prevalent in other sports. Runners, swimmers, bikers, football players, Olympic lifters, professional wrestlers and many other types of athletes partook of the performance-enhancing and muscle-building properties of steroids and other drugs. Strength athletes took the most political and legal flak because with their extreme muscle mass they are by nature the most high-profile steroid users. Walking down the street at 280 pounds wearing spandex and a shirt that reads "Get big or get out of town" does not help matters either for the reputation of the bodybuilding community with the general public.

As the mid-'80s rolled around, the antisteroid juggernaut really took off. Horror story after horror story came out about the "evils" of steroid use and the ability of these drugs to turn normal people into ax murderers from " 'roid rage," assuming the user had not already died of liver failure! The media applied their usual "don't confuse us with the facts" style of journalism to the whole issue of steroids. The lure of a sensational story the world would eat up took precedence over logic, medical experience and published research.

Am I making an argument that steroids are safe drugs devoid of danger and side effects? Absolutely not! I am, however, a stickler for the facts. Emotions can never alter facts, but facts can alter one's emotions. The facts are the facts no matter how people feel morally, ethically or emotionally about steroids, or any other drug for that matter. Steroids are serious medications that can have serious consequences if abused, misused or taken by people with pre-existing medical problems that can be exacerbated by steroids. The fact of the matter is, thousands of different drugs people take every day (which were prescribed by their doctor no less) are far more toxic than steroids.

For example, thousands – perhaps millions – of people take diuretics every day to combat simple problems such as water retention. Some of these drugs (e.g. Lasix) can kill you very easily at dosages not much higher than what is prescribed by the doctor. Good old aspirin kills more than 400 children every year. If you really want to see which drugs are killing people off by the thousands, pick up a copy of the report that is published every year by the Association of Poison Control.

Some male steroid users develop unsightly gynecomastia – a condition commonly referred to as "bitch tits."

On the very first page of his book *Anabolic Steroid Side Effects – Fact, Fiction and Treatment*, Dr. Mauro G. DiPasquale, a noted authority on steroids, states, "As used by most athletes, the side effects of anabolic steroid use appear to be minimal. Even in those using large doses for prolonged periods of time, clinical evidence shows that many of the short-term side effects are mostly reversible. As well, some of the more serious side effects, such as hepatic toxicity and increased serum cholesterol, can be minimized by proper monitoring, changes in lifestyle, and if indicated, medication."

So what's my point? The basis of science and medicine is objective research. The word *objective* is defined by *Webster's College Dictionary* as "not influenced by personal feelings or prejudice; unbiased: an objective opinion." All "good" science is based on objectivity. Unfortunately I would estimate that most of the medical establishment and all

of the general public have lost their objectivity over the subject of steroids. Like abortion, sex education and gun control, steroids have become an emotionally heated topic. It is virtually impossible to find relevant and objective research on steroids any more because researchers are too afraid to conduct any studies for fear of public, political and legal reprisal. I know this to be true because I recently had a conversation with the director of one of the country's largest military research facilities who confessed to me that even he was unable to get steroid research approved. "It's just too hot a political topic right now," he stated. This is a case of the media and public opinion actually affecting scientific and medical research, and that is a very dangerous situation indeed. As with all potentially dangerous drugs (and steroids are potentially dangerous drugs), they should be prescribed by a doctor. Steroids are like any class of drugs. They range from amaz-

Most of the top bodybuilders use anabolic drugs to aid physique development.

era of political correctness where argument and healthy debate are often shunned, anyone who makes a statement alluding to the possibility that steroids are not as dangerous as the media or government would have you believe is tagged as "prosteroid." I am not prosteroid. Period. I am by nature antidrug in general. I am, however, protruth, and the truth goes against what many people hold dear to their heart as morally correct or scientifically accurate. Remember, facts are facts. Whether it is "right" or "wrong" to use drugs (in this case steroids) is a different matter. I do not think most people should use steroids, but if they are going to use steroids, regardless of whether or not you or I approve, they should be able to go to their doctor for a prescription so as to avoid the side effects of ignorance and the bad advice of most black-market steroid dealers. As it stands now, many states have passed laws forbidding doctors from prescribing steroids to athletes, and doctors in other states are too afraid of the repercussions to even monitor the health of most steroid users.

ingly nontoxic to very toxic. Obviously an athlete should be monitored by his or her doctor for signs of potential trouble. If there is a sign of trouble (e.g. unacceptably high liver enzymes or a large rise in cholesterol), the appropriate steps should be taken by the doctor to adjust the dosages, change steroids or take the athlete off the drugs altogether if need be. As the case is now, steroids are purchased out of the trunk of a car from a black-market dealer selling substances of dubious quality and safety.

Steroid use has not gone down one bit. In fact, it has gone up over the past ten years. This is a very sad state of affairs indeed. This "pass a law and stick your head in the sand" logic that is applied to steroid use is far more dangerous to the athletes than the drugs could ever be. When I interviewed a medical researcher for *MuscleMag International* on what he considered to be the most dangerous steroid, he said, "The most dangerous drug is ignorance." I could not have said it better myself. In this new

Yet another fact that seems to elude the purveyors of steroid doom is the use of steroids by the medical community for the treatment of various diseases. At this very moment there is research going on with AIDS patients to see if steroids can be used to stop the muscle-wasting and immune suppression of AIDS, and I know several researchers who are already using steroids on AIDS patients with positive effects. The World Health Organization (WHO) has been carrying out large-scale studies to see if steroids can be used as safe and reversible birth control for men. At dosages similar to those used by many athletes, the studies found no negative long-term side effects. How can steroids be a safe and effective treatment for AIDS patients and a safe form of male birth control, but unhealthful and dangerous for athletes? Is this a biological paradox or an ideologically based hypocrisy?

If there is any one flaw a person of character should find more distasteful than ignorance, it is hypocrisy. Drug use of any kind might be morally "wrong," but is sending mixed messages showing a huge bodybuilder saying, "I did it all with Weight Gainer Nine Million" the correct way to influence our young athletes? Young people can sense hypocrisy as readily as a police dog can sniff out cocaine at the airport. You can't hide anything from people (especially young people), and once they catch you lying to them they will never listen to you again. That's why the current health warnings regarding steroids are falling on deaf ears. Now I am not here to argue the pros and cons of steroids, and I know that nothing I say will sway people in either direction. That's a funny thing about people – once they have set their mind on a position, no amount of arguing, proof or research to the contrary is going to change it. I can live with that. So here's the bottom line:

(1) Steroids can be dangerous drugs, but they are far less dangerous than many of the drugs that are prescribed every day to unwitting Americans.

(2) How dangerous steroids are depends on the dosage, duration and type of steroid being used.

(3) Some people can and will use huge amounts of known-to-be-toxic steroids and will never have a serious side effect, while others will use small amounts of less toxic steroids and will have side effects severe enough to make them stop taking the drugs.

(4) Whether or not a person will experience any short-term or long-term negative side effects depends on genetic factors, diet, additional drug use and a host of other variables that are too numerous for this book. (See the chapter "Avoiding Steroid Side Effects" for more information.)

I will now get off the soap box I find myself perched on, and will get down to the point of this chapter – drug use, then and now. What about all the other high-tech drugs bodybuilders are now using? Well, that's a whole other story. Some of these drugs are relatively innocuous, while others are down-right scary. Modern high-level competitive bodybuilding is chemical assistance at its dare-devil best – chemical Russian roulette so to speak.

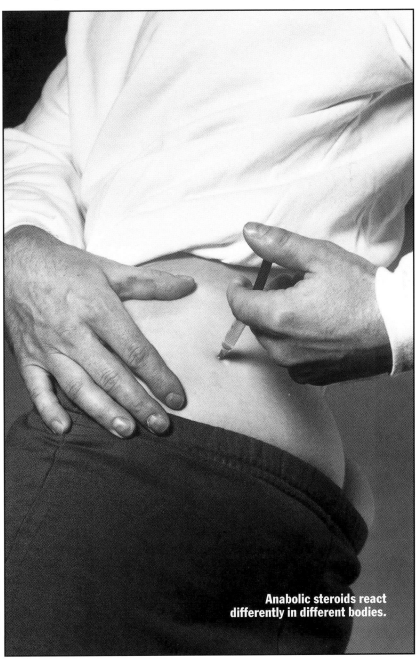

Anabolic steroids react differently in different bodies.

The Good Old Days

I remember walking into a hardcore gym in the early '80s to see some guy in the locker room actually giving himself a shot with about ten guys standing around watching casually as they were getting changed to work out. No one bothered to hide what was going on as I walked in, even though I was a complete stranger to this gym. I had some good muscle on me at the time, and as far as they were concerned, that was all you needed to be above suspicion. Out on the gym floor, perched on a flat bench, they had a small, white Dixie cup filled with D-bol tabs. Virtually anyone could grab a few as though they were candy. "Melt in your mouth, not in your hands," you could say. Back in those days steroids were so cheap and easy to obtain that putting a few hundred D-bol in a cup for your buddies was no big deal. Nowadays, if you were to reach for a person's drug supply that was left out, you would probably get yourself killed. Steroid-taking was pretty basic stuff for the most part. Maybe there were a few people who could use them in a scientific way, but for 99.9 percent of the guys who used steroids, the procedure was basically unscientific and straightforward.

Drugs such as Testosterone Cypionate and Enanthate, EQ, Deca, D-bol, Anavar and Anadrol were the staples in the off-season. Sure, there was always some Primo, Winstrol and Maxibolin floating around, but most people considered these drugs as too wimpy to waste any money on when maximum size was the goal. Today people pretty much take whatever they can get. Of the bodybuilders I knew at the time who were using steroids – and I knew quite a few – many had a doctor's prescription for these drugs. They also had regular blood tests done, not because they were so health conscious, but because the doctor would not prescribe them steroids if they did not get regular blood work done every few months.

The diet was fairly basic too. "Eat everything that doesn't move or scream" was the attitude of most off-season bodybuilders. (Well, maybe if it screamed just a little, it was still OK to eat.) Other than the basic milk-and-egg protein powder, desiccated liver tabs and a multivitamin, there was not much for useful supplements. This combination of drug use, eating and training produced some very large people. Under all that water and fat there was some serious muscle too. When it came to precontest dieting, things went downhill for most bodybuilders. They generally ate too little, trained too much, and did not have access to the high-tech drugs (and people who knew how to use these drugs), supplements and nutritional knowledge that are available today. That is not to say that the majority of today's bodybuilders have a closet full of high-tech drugs, a guru-type trainer to teach them how to use these drugs, and the most scientifically based diet and supplement regimen that money can buy, but they do have more access to this type of information.

I think it is a huge disservice to the modern bodybuilder to say

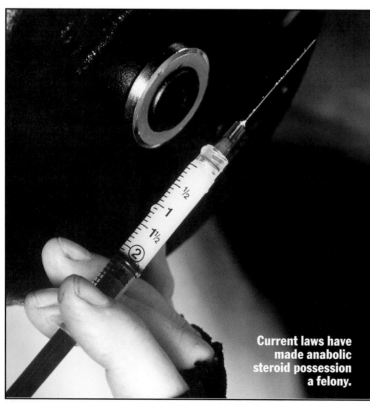

Current laws have made anabolic steroid possession a felony.

Some athletes will go to any lengths to succeed.

that we have better athletes today because we have better drugs. The truth is, we have larger and more ripped bodybuilders because we have much better nutritional knowledge, supplements, training techniques, and more high-tech drugs combined with people who know how to use them. The expression "knowledge is power" says it all in the sport of modern high-level bodybuilding.

Modern Insanity?

I think it is safe to say that no one – but no one – gets into high-level competitive sports to improve his health, and high-level competitive bodybuilding is no exception. For example, if you asked a pro football player whether he got into football because he thought it would be

More dangerous than steroids is ignorance.

stupid TV program or spend the remainder of your life in misery.

In truth, the majority of athletes, including bodybuilders, run into health problems from the use of recreational drugs (cocaine, Nubain, alcohol, etc.), bad diets and high-stress lifestyles. Steroids and other performance-enhancing drugs must be added into the overall equation, but they are rarely the only culprit in the degradation of an athlete's health. Of course, the headline "Athlete Has High Cholesterol and Dies of a Heart Attack" makes for a boring story on the ten o'clock news, so the "Athlete Who Used Steroids for Eight Weeks back in 1978 Dies of Heart Attack" always makes the headlines first. I have been interviewed many times by various TV shows and news programs, and I am always amazed at how well they can manipulate, take out of context or change outright a person's words to get a more interesting story for their viewers. Nonetheless, if you abuse steroids you could pay a high price physically, emotionally and financially. And that ain't no joke.

So what other drugs do modern high-level bodybuilders use besides steroids? Obviously I can't speak for every bodybuilder, but I can report on what I have seen with my own two eyes, and believe me, these two eyes have seen a lot. Below is a list of all the drugs that were used by a national-level bodybuilder who was getting ready for one of the country's most competitive amateur shows. He did have both medical supervision and access to information on how to use these drugs. Two points that should be made here: (1) I know many of these drugs will be unfamiliar to the reader. Good! Don't look them up, and for Christ's sake don't use them. (2) You will notice that I have not put how much of each drug was used, when they were used or how they were used. This is because I have no wish to write a "how to" guide on the various drugs used by

good for his health, he would probably hit you over the head with his helmet at about the same time he broke into laughter at the stupid question. I don't mean to imply that all high-level athletes are unhealthy people, but health is certainly not the reason they are in sports. Modern sports is b-i-i-i-g money. When there are big bucks involved, health usually goes out the window. This is a sad but true aspect of life in our commercialized, dehumanized "win at all costs" society. My opinion, and the advice I give the athletes I work with, is that people have a responsibility to take all possible measures to remain healthy. There is life after bodybuilding. Don't forget this fact. If you throw your health away for a trophy and a fistful of money, you could be another tragic feature story on some

bodybuilders and other athletes. I will tell you this: If you were to find all of these drugs and use them you would (a) end up looking like dirt, (b) be so broke you would not be able to feed yourself, and (c) be lucky to be standing upright!

If you are interested in additional information on steroids and other drugs, I recommend you read *Anabolic Steroid Side Effects – Facts, Fiction and Treatment* and *Beyond Anabolic Steroids*, both written by Dr. DiPasquale, *Anabolic Reference Guide* (6th issue) by Bill Phillips, and *The Underground Steroid Handbook* by Dan Duchaine. These are all good books. I hope I have made myself perfectly clear on this point of safety as it pertains to drug use, but in case I have not, an asterisk appears next to certain drugs. The asterisk means this: Use this drug without extremely close medical supervision and you could die. Whether the other drugs will kill you is debatable, but they are certainly not likely to improve your health. This is an FYI-only list and is not intended as a guide. So without further ado, here is the list.

Sustanon 250
Anavar
Winstrol
Anadrol
Primobolan Depot
Testosterone Propionate
Parabolan
Permastril
Halotestin
Equipoise
Andriol
HCG
Insulin*
GH
Proscar
Nolvadex
Aldactone
Lasix*
EPO*
Clenbuterol
Nubain*
Triacana
Synthroid
Esiclene
Proviron
Teslac
Cytadren

Believe it or not, there are quite a few more drugs that bodybuilders and other athletes might use, but this list is not at all unusual for a high-level precontest bodybuilder "in the know" about what to take and how to take it. In my opinion several of the drugs listed are either redundant, not needed or too dangerous to mess with. For example, Nubain does appear to have cortisol-lowering/anticatabolic effects, but probably will not make any real difference in such a stack, plus it is extremely habit forming, illegal and potentially life threatening. Nubain is a strong painkiller in the morphine family of drugs, and some people use it to "mellow out" or ease joint pains. It has sent more than a few athletes to the drug rehab center, so stay away from it.

Certainly drug use is different for each athlete. Some bodybuilders might use other drugs such as IGF, Cytomel, Dynabolin and test suspension. Use really depends on availability, cost, preference, etc. Many of these drugs were either not invented ten years ago, or were just unknown to athletes. Scary stuff, no? Strangely enough, I have found a much wider difference among athletes' preferences regarding supplements than I have with drugs. Some people will use a huge amount of supplements, while others take no more than a multivitamin. Many of the above drugs are used in varying amounts by athletes other than bodybuilders.

Conclusion

Let us not forget that there is such a creature as a natural bodybuilder – yes, they do exist! – but this chapter is not about natural athletes, now is it? I have worked with many natural bodybuilders and other athletes, and I think natural athletes should get the respect they deserve, but I also believe athletes who use drugs do not necessarily have one foot in the grave or turn into ax murderers. I hope this chapter has enlightened you, informed you and ingrained in your mind the idea that health should always be your number one priority, whether you use steroids or not.

Chapter Eight
Dealing With Steroid Side Effects

It would be nice if nobody used steroids and other drugs to win bodybuilding contests or other various athletic endeavors. A few gifted people in each sport have such perfect genetics for that sport that they need no chemical

Steroids differ in their toxicity.

enhancement to regularly beat other competitors who use drugs. However, this is the exception and not the rule. Athletes who use drugs usually have an edge over natural athletes; otherwise, drugs would not be illegal in sports competitions. It would also be a wonderful world if every athlete who used athletic-enhancing drugs did so with the assistance and care of a *qualified physician* (italics because physicians who know much of anything about steroids are rare). Sadly, this is the real world where bodybuilders and other athletes don't seek medical advice, don't get regular blood tests, and use drugs which they purchase from black-market dealers. Combine this behavior with a poor understanding of the mechanism of action and pharmacology of steroids, and side effects are a given.

It should be noted that there is a wide range of tolerance in all people for different chemicals. Some people can drink large amounts of alcohol and suffer no hangover the next day, while others will drink a small amount and feel like hell warmed over the following morning. I personally cannot drink more than a single cup of coffee without problems, while my friend can take several ephedrine caps and chase them down with half a pot of coffee before a workout with no trouble. Genetic predisposition, medical history, diet, other drug interactions – among many possible factors – all play a part in deciding how the human body will react to steroids and other compounds, or even vitamins and food. One can't accurately predict how a person will react to each steroid, so I will not even try. For a further discussion on this topic, read the chapter "Steroids: Then and Now." It contains more information on the physical and moral ramifications of steroid use.

I will give some general guidelines and observations that might help, but the final decision is up to you and will hopefully be based on truth, accurate information and a long talk with your doctor. The possible legal ramifications of steroid use are obvious, so I won't go any further on that topic, although you should keep it in mind if you use, or are thinking of using, steroids. I also will not beat the proverbial dead horse with a long and boring explanation of every conceivable side effect of steroids and why side effects happen. There are several good books on the subject which I have already mentioned elsewhere (see chapter 7). What this chapter offers, that those books do not, is a more detailed discussion of nutrients, drugs, etc., you can take to offset the most common side effects of these drugs.

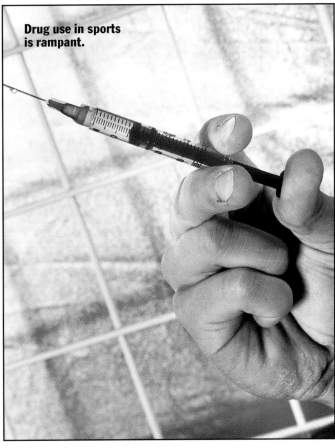

Drug use in sports is rampant.

The highly androgenic steroids such as Anadrol, Parabolan, and the testosterones (to name only a few) tend to be responsible for the majority of serious side effects, but the biochemical individuality of each person is the final dictator of whether or not a person will experience negative side effects. No matter how resistant to the side effects a person is, he can override that resistance with some of the insane dosages and practices of the modern bodybuilder. I think this goes without saying, but I will say it anyway: ALL ATHLETES WHO USE STEROIDS SHOULD GET REGULAR BLOOD TESTS. Although blood tests do not prevent side effects, they can potentially head off any serious long-term complications associated with steroid use. In this chapter I make some recommendations on tactics, supplements and drugs that might be useful for avoiding and/or treating some (but not all!) of the side effects of anabolic steroids. They are not intended as a treatment to be used in place of regular blood tests and the advice of your doctor. To just take some vitamins I recommend, and hope to God they work, would not only be unscientific of you, but it would also be incredibly stupid. If you cannot afford the time or money to get blood tests and pay for the doctor visits – if you think so little of your long-term health – you should not be taking steroids in the first place.

Many bodybuilders are afraid to go to a doctor for blood tests. I am not sure why they feel this way. Doctors will not turn you in to the law for steroid use. No matter how they feel personally about an athlete who uses steroids (or any other drug for that matter) they are bound by the "doctor-patient relationship" and would lose their license if they turned you in. They are not required to give you steroids, but they are required to monitor your health. Of course, a doctor could turn you away for personal reasons, but that means he is a shitty doctor and you don't want to deal with him anyway. Most doctors will just give you the basic lecture on why steroids are bad for you (which they can be) and when they realize they are unable to talk you out of using these drugs, will (hopefully) be willing to monitor your general health.

If the doctor is able to talk you out of using the drugs, good for him! Considering today's climate regarding the legality of steroids and the lack of safe clean drugs, you would probably be best off avoiding steroids altogether, but if you have set your mind on using them I certainly won't be able to change it. Unlike the medical community and society, I won't turn my back on you because I am unable to talk you

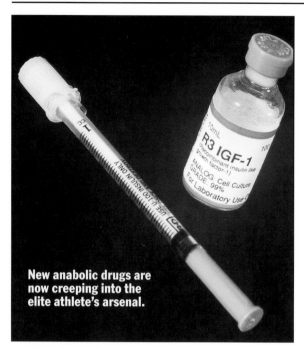

New anabolic drugs are now creeping into the elite athlete's arsenal.

out of using steroids. So if you are one of those people, this chapter is for you.

When you go to get blood tests, be honest with your doctor. There is no reason to go there if you are going to lie to him (or her) as he stares at a blood test that shows your liver enzymes are off the scale and your cholesterol is 320! Don't forget, several of the liver enzyme tests can be high in natural bodybuilders also, and are a result of the breakdown of tissue and/or a high-protein diet typical of bodybuilders. Some doctors are aware of this fact and some are not. For example, the SGOT and SGPT are commonly high in natural bodybuilders and powerlifters. There are other liver functions that are affected by intense weight training and a high-protein diet, but as I said in the beginning of this chapter, I am not going to go into great detail about the bio-chemistry of steroid side effects and blood tests because there is plenty of good information already written on the topic.

My best advice is to find a doctor you can work with and give him a copy of any one of the books I mentioned in previous chapters. I would recommend in particular Dr. DiPasquale's book on side effects because (a) it is the most detailed book on the subject of steroid side effects, though probably a bit too technical for most people to understand, and (b) it is written by a doctor and will get more respect from your

doctor, as doctors can be quite snobbish about whom they take advice from. Also, I recommend you always ask for a copy of your blood test so you can take a look at it at home. They really are not very hard to read, though the doctor should be the final interpreter of the blood tests. The doctor will usually look at you as if you have no right to ask him for a copy of your own blood test, but that is his (or her) tough shit. It's your health and your blood test, so don't be intimidated by the doctor. As for which tests you should get, how often you should get them and what each test means, I will leave that to your doctor's discretion, or you can find the test recommendations in the books listed in chapter 7. Below are some of the most common side effects and what you can do about them.

General Advice for Avoiding Steroid Side Effects

(1) Stay off the drugs for at least as long as you stay on them.
(2) It is better to mix small to moderate amounts of different steroids than it is to take large amounts of a single steroid.
(3) Don't mix steroids high in androgens (i.e. testosterones, Anadrol, Halotestin, etc.). If using steroids high in androgens, use only one per cycle mixed with low-androgen steroids and keep the steroid that is high in androgens to a moderate dosage.
Acne: See chapter 9.
Baldness (hair loss): discussed at length in chapter 9.

Common Side Effects

Cholesterol increase/heart disease: In certain individuals cholesterol will go up during steroid use. A rise in total cholesterol is not as important as a change in the ratio of your LDL (bad cholesterol) to HDL (the good cholesterol). Although exercise often improves the HDL-to-LDL ratio, steroids can offset that benefit. Only blood tests will tell you what is going on. If your HDL drops dramatically when you're using steroids, and it remains that way for a prolonged time, you could be seriously jeopardizing your health, yet the HDL levels usually go back to normal after you stop using the drugs. What most people don't know is that total cholesterol is a poor indicator of heart-disease risk.

Many people who have low cholesterol have heart attacks while many other people who have high cholesterol will never have heart disease. Fat has gotten a bad rap in the causes of heart disease and other diseases (see chapter 4). Certain dietary fats can cause heart disease while others prevent heart disease and/or treat it. In truth, high cholesterol and the pathology of heart disease result from a complex interaction among certain types of fats, carbohydrates, a lack of antioxidants in the diet, and many other factors. This entire subject is far too broad and complex for this chapter or this book, but a more detailed discussion on fats can be found in other chapters.

The ultimate cause of heart disease is the oxidation of cholesterol to plaque (Anon. "Out-'FOX'ing Cholesterol Tests?" *Science,* 1994). Plaque (the hard stuff that clogs your arteries) is nothing more than oxidized LDL cholesterol. Although mainstream medicine clings furiously to its "high fat in the diet causes high cholesterol and high cholesterol causes heart disease" stance, research has disproven this position repeatedly. Research has continuously shown that antioxidants can dramatically reduce the risk of heart disease, cancer and many other diseases. In fact, one very large study showed the most accurate predictor of heart disease is your serum vitamin E. The amount of vitamin E in the blood was found to be much more reliable than total cholesterol in predicting whether people would get heart disease. I could put down a whole list of references – and I have virtually hundreds of studies – to back up my claim, but in my opinion it is an established scientific fact and listing references would be a waste of time.

However, there is plenty of evidence showing saturated fat and/or cholesterol are not the cause of heart disease. For instance: (a) There have been 33 clinical trials that have failed to show that saturated fat intake or cho-

lesterol is related to heart disease. (b)The Framingham study, which ran for 40 years on a large population, failed to show that saturated fat intake was related to heart disease. (c)The Masai tribespeople eat far more saturated fat and cholesterol than Americans and do not suffer from heart disease. (d)The Inuit diet is more than 60 percent fat (from whale blubber), yet heart disease is virtually unknown to them. Only after the Inuit changed to a western diet did their rate of heart disease soar. (e)Last but not least, although heart disease has gone up astronomically over the past 100 years in the US, our intake of cholesterol has not changed. The heart-disease rate in the US went up dramatically when we started eating more processed liquid vegetable oils and hydrogenated oils and less saturated fat. These are just a few of many examples showing that we are being duped by mainstream medicine and the media into supporting the low-fat/no-fat multibillion-

Drug use can often spoil a bodybuilder's aesthetics.

dollar industry that has sprung up to cash in on Americans' fat phobia.

If you want to prevent heart disease and possibly lower your cholesterol (whether you use steroids or not), take a good multi-vitamin/multimineral and about 800-1000 I.U. of vitamin E and 3-6 grams a day of buffered vitamin C, to prevent the LDL from oxidizing and possibly raise HDL. Stay away from the "bad" fats (see chapter 4) and avoid too much simple sugar or an overly high-carbohydrate diet. Take 1-3 tablespoons of flax oil (the good fat) daily for all the reasons discussed in the chapter on fats. If you are particularly interested in this topic, write to me at my post-office box and I will try to send you a list of references you can look up on the subject.

Gynecomastia (bitch tits): Just about every bodybuilder and his mother knows that many steroids convert to estrogen through the pro-cess of aromatization which causes a swelling of the breast tissue known as "bitch tits." Taking large amounts of low-androgen steroids or moderate to large amounts of steroids high in androgens causes this affliction, though not all steroids high in androgens aromatize to estrogen. Again, biochemical individuality seems to play a large part in whether a person will develop bitch tits. Some people can take enough Anadrol to turn their eyes yellow (not a good situation) but will not develop "gyno," while other people will start to develop gyno from even looking at a box of Anadrol. Some bodybuilders take Nolvadex, an antiestrogen, to prevent or control the gynecomastia. Sometimes this strategy works and sometimes it does not. If the gyno does not go away, many bodybuilders have it surgically removed.

Recently, however, I have come across a possible way to reduce or eliminate the gyno. I actually made this discovery by accident. Several bodybuilders I know who take flax oil or the more balanced blend made by Flora (known as Udo's Choice Ultimate Oil Blend) for all the reasons I mention in chapter 4 have reported a reduction or a disappearance of their gyno. At first I put this result down to coincidence, but after a half-dozen or so bodybuilders reported similar experiences, I started to think about it and decided it does make a certain amount of sense. The hard lump that forms under the nipple is actually a type of benign tumor. Many studies have shown omega-3 fatty acids (of which flax oil is the richest source) to be useful for eliminating solid tumors, and many medical doctors who practice progressive nutritionally based medicine have had good results in using flax oils with cancer patients. This effect on gynecomastia only seems to happen at higher intakes of about four to five or more tablespoons a day.

Obviously I can't guarantee this method will work for you if you have gynecomastia, and the science on this one is admittedly shaky, but it could be worth a try. If you use flax oil or the Udo's Choice oil, you should start out at one tablespoon a day mixed in a protein drink and work your way up slowly over a month or so. Wait a few months to see if you get any results. Then work your way back down to one to three tablespoons a day as a maintenance dosage. Of course, if you are using steroids you know to

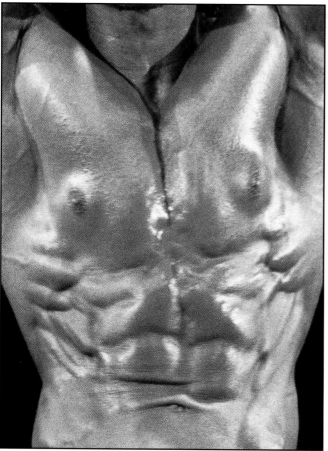

Gynecomastia (bitch tits) certainly detracts from a competitor's physique.

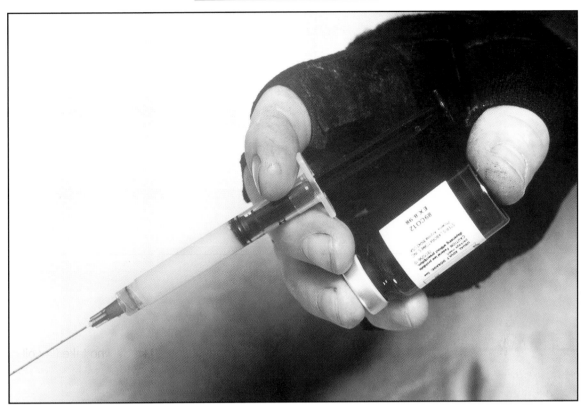

cause bitch tits while you are taking flax oil, they will probably offset any positive results the flax oil would have on the gyno.

Liver toxicity: Oral steroids seem to be the worst offenders when it comes to liver toxicity. Those of the 17a-alkylated variety (i.e. Anadrol and others) are more often than not the culprits. However, even small amounts of steroids that are considered to be fairly nontoxic can elevate liver enzymes in particularly sensitive individuals. This fact brings us back to our old friend, the concept of "biochemical individuality." Although raised liver enzymes are not always an indicator of liver dysfunction, they should never be ignored by the athlete. The primary cause of liver toxicity from steroids is probably the inflammation (secondary to free-radical production) and a reduction of the protective fatty acids that are found in the liver, which can lead to more serious complications if left untreated. Oral steroids are chemically modified to resist being destroyed during digestion. This modification appears to be stressful to the liver.

The use of antioxidants, of which there are many different types, has been shown to be protective of the liver in both a preventative and

The manner in which many athletes use steroids could be described as abusive.

therapeutic manner. Antioxidants such as vitamins C and E and selenium have acted as strong hepato protectants. Several herbs such as silymarin (milk thistle extract) and licorice have strong liver-protectant, antioxidant and anti-inflammatory properties. Flax oil and/or evening primrose oil (see chapter 4 for more information) are also used by bodybuilders to replace the essential fatty acids that are depleted in the liver by the use of oral steroids. There are many more antioxidants, herbs and drugs that have been found to help with liver toxicity of all kinds, such as those resulting from alcohol use, steroid use and chemical poisoning, but these are the ones most commonly used by bodybuilders. I would recommend these vitamins and herbs as preventative measures when taking steroids, but don't use them as an excuse not to get those blood tests. Other benefits of taking the above nutrients are a possible reduction in cholesterol, improved recuperation, resistance to various diseases and decreased joint pain, to name only a few.

Prostate enlargement: See chapter 9.

Chapter Nine
The Big Three and DHT
Hair Loss, Acne and Prostate Enlargement

I know what you are thinking: "What could male pattern baldness, zits, and – God forbid – prostate enlargement possibly have in common?" As you will find out shortly, they have a great deal in common. At first glance grouping these afflictions together might seem strange, but further inquiry into the mechanism behind these three "side effects of life" (as my old physiology professor would call them) will explain why I have lumped them together in this chapter.

Proscar can help reduce the conversion of testosterone to DHT but at a cost.

Although these maladies can have numerous causes and resulting treatments, there is a single factor that is usually responsible. (Bear with me – I am getting to the good part.) Hair loss and acne are not life threatening, but they can cause great psychological distress for many people. Prostate enlargement, on the other hand, is something to be concerned about and should never be ignored. Women do not have prostates, so this is obviously not going to be a problem for them, although they can experience hair loss (especially if they are using steroids) and acne. As the media has spent so much time reminding us, anabolic/androgenic steroids can initiate or generally exacerbate these conditions. However, it should not be assumed that because you use steroids you will have these problems, or by not using steroids you will avoid them. Some steroid-using athletes seem to avoid these side effects, while others – users and nonusers – suffer one or more of these conditions. The result mostly depends on their genetic predisposition (i.e. biochemical individuality), which is the part the media conveniently leaves out. In truth, very few young men who do not use steroids have enlarged prostates. I wish I could say the same about their counterparts.

The Culprit

The cause, or the common link, of all this is a hormone with the long name of dihydro-testosterone (DHT). DHT is converted in the body from testosterone (and other androgens) by an enzyme called 5-alpha-reductase. Conversion of DHT from testosterone by this enzyme system is considered to be the main culprit, or environmental trigger, of these afflictions. Testosterone can also undergo irreversible conversion to estrogen (17 beta-estradoil), which has its own positive and negative (mostly negative) effects. To make a long story short, when DHT binds with receptor sites in the skin, it makes the sebaceous glands produce more oil. Combine this increase with the interaction of bacteria, dried skin, etc., and you have acne.

Although recent discoveries have shown DHT is not the final cause of hair loss, DHT causes the follicle to stop growing hair (known as the "resting phase"). We know that men who are predisposed to male-pattern baldness have much greater concentrations of DHT and androgen affinity in the hair follicles that are being affected – i.e. areas that are losing hair. Conversely, men who are found to have congenitally low 5-alpha-reductase levels show no receding of the hairline. The complete mechanism to prostate enlargement has not been figured out, but it is well established that DHT plays a major role and interacts with other hormones in a complex fashion that has yet to be fully explained. Men commonly experience some prostate enlargement as they age because of this build-up of DHT. With approximately 400,000 prostatectomies per year in the US alone, this is a serious problem for many men.

It is important to note (for reasons that will be made clearer later) that there are two types of the enzyme that convert testosterone to DHT – 5-alpha-reductase type 1, which is found in the skin, and type 2, which is found in the prostate.

Below is a summary of the desirable effects of testosterone and the undesirable effects of DHT:

Testosterone:
*Male sex drive, performance
*Muscle mass increases
*Bodyfat decreases
*Sperm production

DHT
*Hair loss (on scalp)
*Hair growth (face and body)
*Acne
*Prostate enlargement

The Juice

Where does the "juice" fit into all this? It should be obvious from the above list what, and why, these things happen when a person injects testosterone. Other steroids vary in their ability to convert to DHT. Drugs high in androgens such as methandrostenolone (Dianabol) and oxymetholone (Anadrol) also convert readily to DHT. This is why people using these drugs keep checking their hairline in the mirror and keep their T-shirt on to cover up the acne. Drugs that do not convert easily into DHT such as oxandrolone (Anavar), nandrolone decanoate (Deca-Durabolin) and nandrolone phenpropionate (Durabolin) do not have a pronounced effect on hair loss, acne and prostate enlargement if taken in reasonable dosages. Some have suggested that steroids that are derived from DHT (but don't convert to DHT if used in moderate amounts), such as stanozolol (Winstrol) and methenolone (Primobolan), can also cause DHT-related side effects, but this does not appear to be the case. Anecdotal evidence points more toward the androgen content of the compound rather than its source derivative. This is only a generalization, however, as there are high-androgen steroids that do not convert to DHT, and vice versa. It's really a drug-by-drug situation.

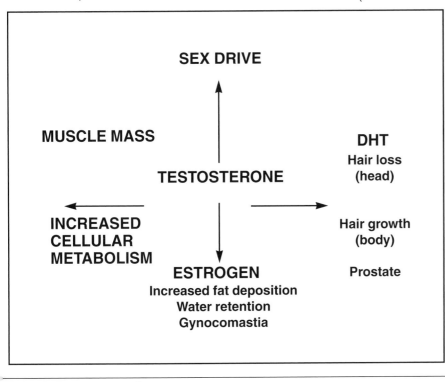

The Good News

Topical solutions for hair loss such as minoxidil, polysorbate 80, topical androgens and other remedies have met with only limited success, but can be better than nothing. Topically applied medications for acne such as Retin-A work to some degree but have draw-backs such as causing red itchy skin, and antibiotics and Accutane cannot be taken indefinitely. Most treatments for prostate enlargement are more of a sentence than a remedy. None of these strategies addresses the underlying problem, which is, of course, the DHT. Here we have the dilemma. Lower a man's testosterone and he might grow some hair, decrease an enlarged prostate or improve his acne, but at what cost? Less muscle, more fat and a disinterest in sex? No thanks! Definitely not conducive to growing

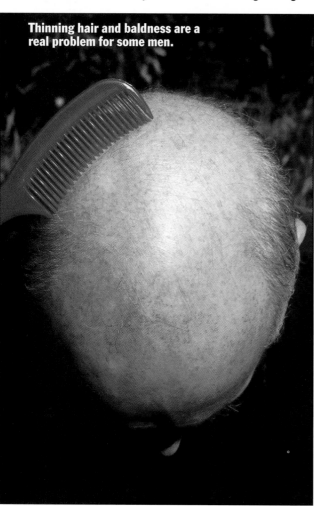

Thinning hair and baldness are a real problem for some men.

muscle. If you increase your testosterone (e.g. your androgens), naturally or otherwise, you face a host of other problems I have already mentioned, and a few I have not. What to do?

The key to this problem is a class of drugs and naturally derived compounds called "alpha-reductase inhibitors." As the name implies, they inhibit the enzyme that converts testosterone to DHT. There are several of these compounds in use already, with several more under investigation. One such drug is Proscar. Unfortunately Proscar has side effects such as impotence, loss of sex drive (5 percent and 3 percent respectively), and headaches in a small number of users. The number of men who experience these problems is low, but that won't be much comfort if you are one of them. I have yet to meet any bodybuilders, or receive any letters from bodybuilders and other athletes, complaining of these side effects, but I thought you might want to know that there are some potential risks, although they are admittedly quite rare. Besides, if you tell a bodybuilder he has a 90 percent chance of side effects with a certain drug, he will immediately assume he's going to be among the 10 percent who do not experience any side effects!

Another point that should be made regarding Proscar and Permixon (see below for more info on Permixon) is that both of these compounds can raise estrogen levels and aggravate gynecomastia if taken in large dosages. As you already know from reading this chapter, testosterone can convert to DHT and/or estrogen. If you block the conversion to DHT through the use of Proscar and possibly Permixon, you can get a rise in estrogen because the testosterone-to-DHT pathway is blocked. I have not seen this problem in people using 5 mg per day or less, but above 5 mg per day it could be a problem. The "more is better" attitude common with bodybuilders is not the way to approach reductase inhibitors. In fact, several studies have shown 1 or 2 mg per day of Proscar to be just as effective as 5 mg in reducing DHT. Because Proscar has been found to be predominantly a type 2 reductase inhibitor, with less of an effect on type 1- 5-alpha-reductase, it was postulated that Proscar would probably be more effective for prostate enlargement than it is for hair loss and acne. However, recent research has shown

Proscar to be moderately effective for hair loss, and it is definitely useful when combined with other products used to stop hair loss (see below for more info).

An extract of the saw palmetto plant (Permixon), which has been studied extensively in Europe, has been found to be a moderate to strong (depending on which study you read) inhibitor of type 1 and possibly type 2 alpha-reductase without serious side effects. Permixon has been studied mostly for its effect on prostate enlargement, but one could reasonably conclude it could (should?) have similar success with acne and hair loss. How much success – and at what rate – is not clear, but the preliminary evidence looks promising. It might also be useful in female hirsutism (unwanted facial hair growth), though Proscar would probably be even better for this purpose. Although Permixon has been found to have some 5-alpha-reductase inhibiting properties (with some debate), recent discoveries indicate that much of its effect is through blocking the uptake of DHT and testosterone into the cell combined with strong anti-inflammatory properties. A second plant-product extract called pygeum africanum has been found to have similar, though slightly different, properties without side effects. Proscar is a very specific inhibitor of 5-alpha-reductase. These naturally derived plant products appear to also have some reductase-inhibiting properties coupled with receptor-blocking and anti-inflammatory abilities. In my personal experience, combined with some recent research and feedback from users, Proscar is the product of choice for hair loss while the combination of Permixon and pygeum is more successful for treating an enlarged prostate.

You have probably heard of someone being advised by a dermatologist to try zinc for his acne. Zinc has also been found to have alpha-reductase-inhibiting properties. I know of only one company that is marketing a combination of saw palmetto/pygeum and zinc in the specific European recommended dosage, though there may be others. This product is available through the Life Extension Foundation. You can call them at 1-800-841-5433 for more information on this product or to place an order, and you don't even need a prescription. To obtain Proscar you will need a prescription.

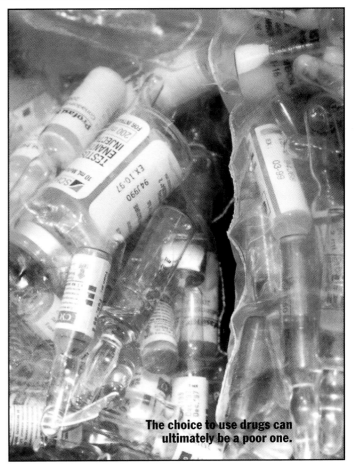

The choice to use drugs can ultimately be a poor one.

DHT Is Not the Main Culprit of Hair Loss.

Until a short time ago researchers thought that DHT was the main cause of hair loss. Further inquiries into the mechanism of hair loss has shown DHT to be an important link in the chain of events that lead to hair loss, but not the direct cause. The final cause of hair loss appears to be an immune rejection by the body against its own hair follicles. The DHT causes a change in the follicles (by yet unknown mechanisms) which causes the body's immune system to see the affected hair follicles as a foreign invader which it then attacks and destroys. At that point your hair starts falling out. How do we know this? Researchers discovered that drugs (such as Cyclosporine) used to suppress the immune system during

Is that extra few pounds of muscle worth the risk?

ulate heart blood flow, and grow hair, to mention only a few of its functions. We now believe that minoxidil works through this pathway. A number of products containing nitric oxide are produced for hair loss. Dr. Peter Proctor makes several such products that have also received good feedback from many users. They can be purchased by calling 713-960-1616.

The Bottom Line On Growing Hair

Why do I go into such great detail about hair loss? If you're like me, you would rather die in a flaming airplane crash than lose your hair. My extensive research into hair loss is for personal reasons. Both my mother's father and my father (and his father before him) lost their hair at a relatively early age. Through the use of the above products I have been able to keep most of my hair on my head, though I have recently added several new products to the mix in hopes they will further grow my hair back. So what if the money I spend on my hair each month exceeds my car-loan payment? I would much rather drive a modest car with a decent head of hair than drive a fancy car with a bald head. There are some men (though very few women) who don't really care about their hair loss, and I respect them for that, but I am not one of those men.

My experience has been that no single product works all that well, but each will help moderately with hair loss. Only when you mix several do you start to see some real hair growth on all but the most stubborn heads. Of course, the earlier you start the better, as growing hair on a bald head is next to impossible. I use a combination of Proscar, minoxidil, NaNo shampoo (made by Dr. Proctor) and Thymuskin. I have only recently (as of 5/28/96) added in the Thymuskin so I can't give any personal feedback as of this writing. The Proscar takes care of the DHT, the minoxidil and NaNo shampoo take care of the NO, and the Thymuskin takes care of the immune rejection. If you have mild hair loss, using any one product might be all you

organ transplants are also very effective for growing hair. They also found that, when viewed through the microscope, the affected hair follicle looks identical to immune rejection seen during organ transplants. This discovery has led researchers to modify the theory on what actually causes hair loss.

Several new products that address the immune rejection have appeared and are having some success at regrowing hair on some people. Among them are Thymuskin and Viviscal. No one is sure how they work, but the feedback I have gotten seems very positive. There is a decent amount of research on both products. They can be purchased from the M.P.B. Buyers' Club by calling 305-758-3173.

Another recent discovery about the mechanism of hair growth and hair loss is its relationship to nitric oxide (NO). NO is a very important mediator of blood-vessel dilation and is needed for men to achieve erections, reg-

need, but if you have severe hair loss (due to genetics and/or steroid use), or, like me, are particularly paranoid about losing your hair, you should probably combine several of them.

Some people might ask, "Hey, Will, how do you know which product is working if you are using three or four different ones at the same time?" My answer to them is always the same: "I don't care which one is working as long as I am growing hair!" If you are losing your hair and don't care about it, that's your business. If you do care, I have given you the option of doing something about it. I never said it would be a cheap option.

Conclusion

The use of alpha-reductase inhibitors will soon play a major role in the treatment and prevention of benign prostatic hyperplasia, acne and hair loss. What role they can play for the bodybuilder (natural and otherwise) is still up in the air, though reductase inhibitors appear to have great potential. However, you have to realize that this is still a fairly new treatment for these problems, so I can't make any guarantees as to their effectiveness. As with all drugs, vitamins, etc., there will probably be a wide range of results for different people. Hair loss, acne and (occasionally) prostate enlargement are common complaints of bodybuilders who use steroids high in androgens. If you want to keep your hair on your head (and your body out of jail), I would avoid them. Low-androgen steroids, though better for your health, involve no less jail time!

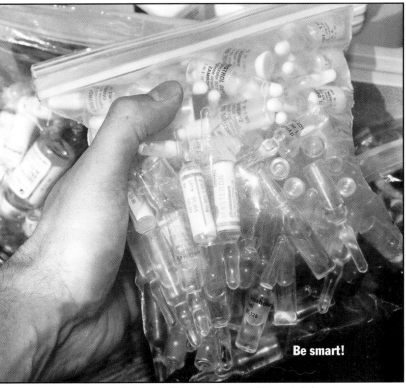

Be smart!

The Best Eighty Bucks I ever Spent!

Besides the cost of my word processor and my twelve-year-old Mazda, the eighty dollars I spent for a membership to the Life Extension Foundation is the best investment I ever made. The Life Extension Foundation is a nonprofit organization dedicated to relevant research from all over the world pertaining to health, disease, performance and a longer life. They market and design products under the strictest standards, and sell them to members at substantial discounts. Much of the money they make is used tirelessly fighting the FDA (Food and Drug Administration), which is hell bent on taking away the right of Americans to free choice with regard to unbiased information and vitamins. This might be a little off the subject, but it is information worth noting.

Bibliography
Schweikert and Wilson, "Regulation of Human Hair Growth by Steroid Hormones, I. Testosterone Metabolism in Isolated Hairs," *Journal of Clinical Endocrinology.* Metab. 38(5): 811-819; 1974.

Carilla, E., Briley, M., Fauren, F., et al., "Binding of Permixon, a new treatment for prostatic benign hyperplasia, to the cytosolic androgen receptor in the rat prostate." *Journal of Steroid Biochem.*, 20: 251-253; 1984.

DiPasquale, M.G., *Anabolic Steroid Side Effects - Fact, Fiction and Treatment.* M.G.D. Press, Warkworth, Ontario Canada., p32–35, 44–46, 62–63; 1990.

Physician's Guide to Life Extension Drugs. Life Extension Press, Fort Lauderdale, FL, pl05-110i 1992.

Additional Sources
Physician's Desk Reference (48th Edition), Medical Economics Data Production Company, Montvale, NJ, 1994.

Hole Jr., J.W., Wm., *Human Anatomy and Physiology* (Fifth Edition), C. Brown Publishers, Dubuque, IA, 1990.

Chapter Ten
Putting It All Together

I realize that I have thrown a great deal of information at the reader. Although it is important that you fully understand the previous chapters, you don't have to grasp all the technical jargon, only know how to apply the information to your personal strategy for gaining muscle. If you do not grasp everything you have just read, or you have forgotten a portion of it (easy to do), go back and read it again. The following chapters contain some of the most effective routines for particular bodyparts, but no routine in the world will ever make up for the wrong diet or poor training habits that are so common among bodybuilders. From your reading so far (before you go on to the routines for legs, back, chest, arms and calves), you should have learned:

• How to present yourself in the best possible manner to make a professional impression on people in the bodybuilding industry, assuming you plan to make money from the fitness industry (see chapter 1).

• How to be prepared for a bodybuilding contest, assuming you have competed or plan to compete in the future (see chapter 2).

• To base your workouts on compound multi-joint movements (i.e. squats, deadlifts, bent rows, dumbell presses, etc.) working the large muscle groups of the legs, back and chest for the maximum endocrine response (see chapter 3).

• Not to stay in the gym longer than an hour (though less time would be even better); to keep training volume low and intensity high if maximum size is the goal (see chapter 3). Although training volume is somewhat of an individual thing, 8 to 12 sets for large bodyparts and 6 to 8 sets for small bodyparts is a good rule of thumb. Overtraining is the number one reason 90 percent of all bodybuilders stop making progress.

• Not to train more than three or four days per week for maximum size, to keep catabolic (muscle-wasting) hormones low and anabolic hormones high (see intro and chapter 3).

• To vary rep ranges and rest time between sets from workout to workout, week to week, or month to month (see chapter 3).

• To avoid stress, stressful situations and boneheads who stress you out, to keep catabolic hormones low (see chapter 3).

• Which carbs to eat, when to eat them, and how much of them to eat, to manipulate insulin levels without getting fat (see chapter 3).

• Which proteins to eat, when to

Amy
Fadhli

eat them and how much you should eat to maintain positive nitrogen levels, IGF levels, thyroid hormones, and improve health and resistance to disease (see chapters 3 and 5).

•Which additional supplements to add if you have the extra money to spend (see chapter 3).

• Which fats to eat, which fats not to eat and how much fat you should eat for maximum size and improved health (see chapters 3 and 4).

• Which vitamins, minerals and other nutrients you should take to improve insulin sensitivity, improve recuperation, avoid heart disease and other degenerative diseases, and improve overall health (see chaps. 3, 4, 8).

• How a high-quality fat-burning supplement is made, how to avoid poorly made fat-burning supplements, and what ingredients should be present in a high-quality fat-burning supplement (see chapter 6).

• How to generally avoid and/or treat anabolic steroid side effects if you insist on using steroids (see chapters 8 and 9).

You might have noticed that nowhere in this book have I mentioned aerobics. I do not think that a blanket "one size fits all" recommendation can be made when it comes to aerobics. Personal experience, anecdotal evidence and most of the research have shown that strength gains are generally hindered by aerobics if they're done in excess. The problem is, what is just right for one person can be excessive to another person, and depends on such variables as drug use, genetics, diet and other compounding factors.

Research indicates that lifting weights does not present a problem for endurance sports (weight training actually improves endurance), but aerobic endurance-type exercise definitely cuts into the size and strength gains of strength athletes. If you are naturally lean but have a tough time putting on size, stay away from any aerobic exercise when trying to gain muscle. If you are the type of person who gets fat easily even when you are eating a good diet, do absolutely as little aerobics as you need to keep relatively lean (i.e. 8 to 12 percent bodyfat for men and 10 to 14 percent for women) and not a drop more. If you fall somewhere between the two groups, as most people do, you will have to experiment with your aerobics schedule. I have found that very few people, unless they are

Dennis Newman

particularly genetically gifted, can add muscle while doing more than three or four 40-minute sessions per week of aerobics. Several of the bodybuilders I have worked with who have won national-level titles have done less than three to four hours total of aerobics per week. If you are eating the correct foods in the correct amounts, taking the right supplements and training correctly, you should need very little aerobics to stay moderately lean while you are trying to gain muscle mass.

This book concerns itself with gaining size, not with getting ripped. That's why I don't refer much to precontest diets, supplements and training strategies. Precontest is a whole different ball of wax and would take up a whole book by itself, so I have not even attempted to discuss it beyond chapter 2. Besides, I need to keep a few tricks up my sleeve, now don't I?

Gerard Dente

Similarly I have not discussed how many calories a person should eat or what percentage each component should make up in the diet. If you paid close attention to the past few chapters, you should have come to the logical conclusion that building muscle is not about calories but about nutrients. Supply all your needs for macronutrients (proteins, carbs, fats) and micronutrients (vitamins, minerals) in the correct amounts at the right times of the day, and the calorie problem will take care of itself. For example, a 200-pound bodybuilder eating 1.5 grams of protein per pound of bodyweight (= 1200 calories) and 2 grams of carbs per pound of bodyweight (= 1600 calories) would have a total of 2800 calories. Add to that number

the fat calories (fat = 9 calories per gram) from a few tablespoons of flax oil, red meat, egg yolks or other foods mentioned previously that he should be eating, and he will easily be somewhere around 3500 to 4000 calories. This is more than sufficient to supply all the energy and growth needs of a 200-pound bodybuilder. Obviously the figures would be different for each person, depending on his bodyweight and the recommendations from chapters 3 and 6.

Remember that nutrient density, not calorie quantity, is the most important factor to growing muscle. Unfortunately most of our foods today are calorie dense and nutrient poor, so you will have to make wise decisions when picking your foods for maximum size gains with minimum fat accumulation. An adequate calorie intake is important, but if those calories are devoid of the proper nutrients (i.e., calorie dense but nutrient poor) you can forget about adding quality muscle. As for what percentage of protein, carbs and fats should make up the daily diet, that will again depend on several different variables. This is why I generally don't feel comfortable making blanket recommendations on macronutrient dietary percentages. A diet of 40 percent protein, 20 to 30 percent fat and 30 to 40 percent carbs is probably the best percentage split for the bodybuilder trying to gain size and minimize fat accumulation, but those numbers can change in response to many factors that have already been noted.

What about the high-carb, low-fat diet, you ask? Again, going into great detail about how and why high-carb, low-fat diets don't work would take a whole book in itself (I am working on it as you read this), but I am sure the reader of this book has a pretty good idea from the foregoing chapters of just how important certain fats are to your health and performance. To put it simply: *The high-carb, low-fat diet is not the optimal diet for bodybuilders!* There are some good fats and there are some bad fats (see chapter 4). Like protein and carbs, not all fats are created equal. Anyone who still pushes the high-carb, low-fat diet either never took a decent biochemistry course or else he slept through it. Even a rudimentary understanding of the biochemical pathways by which protein, carbs and fats are utilized, metabolized and stored will show you why the high-carb, low-

Paul
Dillett

fat/no-fat approach to gaining muscle, losing fat and improving health a complete waste of time. Mr. Duchaine, Dr. DiPasquale, I, and other proponents of the lower-carb, higher-fat approach might disagree slightly on exactly what percentage carbs, fats and proteins should make up in the diet, but they (we) unanimously dislike the high-carb, low-fat way of thinking that is so popular today and continues to produce ever fatter Americans.

Melissa
Coates

fat/no-fat approach is one of the worst possible ways of trying to gain muscle and lose fat. Some of the truly advanced thinkers in body-building and sports nutrition, such as Dr. Mauro DiPasquale, Dr. Barry Sears, Dan Duchaine – and dare I add myself to this list? – to mention only a few names, consider the high-carb, low-

Chapter Eleven

The Three-Way Back Attack

Have you ever wondered, or argued with your friends, what bodypart is the most decisive for winning the big competitions? What bodypart makes or breaks a bodybuilder as he climbs the competitive ladder, or what bodypart really stands out at the beach, on the street or at the gym to separate a true bodybuilder from a wannabe? For my money it is the back. A great back is the true equalizer at any contest. Great chests, huge arms and swept quads are a dime a dozen these days, but a truly impressive back is still a rare sight to behold.

Whenever you study magazine photo coverage of a competition or attend a contest, you notice that the top five people always look great from the front, but when they turn around, the first-place winner becomes instantly apparent by his (or her) back development. The most obvious example was Lee Haney. Many competitors could match Lee in a side chest pose, front double-biceps pose or leg pose, but when Lee hit a front lat spread or a back double-biceps shot, second place was the best anyone else could hope for. Lee's back in particular allowed him to rule bodybuilding for eight years. Today's top stars are no different. Take Dorian Yates and Flex Wheeler for example. All of their bodyparts are great, but their back development is out of this world, and it keeps them ahead of the pack. That's proof enough for me, and I hope for you, that the back is the key bodypart for anyone who wants to be, or at least look like, a competitive bodybuilder.

Unfortunately the back is probably the

Aaron Baker, Flex Wheeler and Dave Fisher

most complex of all bodyparts to train because it is such a complicated muscle group. You have the latissimus dorsi, rhomboideus, infraspinatus, teres major, teres minor, trapezius and many more. This interwoven network of muscles is beautiful in its design and function. Too bad they're all on our back where we can't see them more often!

Form Troubles

Before we can even begin to talk about back training, we have to discuss the atrocious form you can regularly see so many people using. Bad form during chest might still build you decent pecs. Bad form during legs might still build you a decent set of quads. Bad form during shoulders might grow you some delts. But bad form during back-training will just give you a bad lower back and pumped up biceps.

The other day I saw this guy, who could not have weighed more than 180, doing shrugs with what had to be close to 700 pounds. Although he thought he was doing shrugs with this weight, he looked more like a person standing still swinging his head around like some kind of gooney bird. I asked him a simple question: "Can you squat that much weight?" To which he replied, "I can barely squat half that much weight." So I put what seemed at the time to be another simple question: "If your thighs can't move that much weight, what makes you think your traps can?" He muttered a couple of words that started with the letter "f" and walked off. Here's a good rule of thumb: Don't try to shrug anything you can't squat! (Note: Though technically a muscle of the back, traps are generally best trained with shoulders or chest because back-training is so taxing on the system. That is why you won't see trap-training in this chapter. The anecdote simply made a good example of poor form commonly used.)

But seriously, do you get as good a pump in your back as you do in other bodyparts? Are you sore where you want to be? Are your biceps and lower back the sorest muscles after your back day? If you answered "no" to the first two questions and "yes" to the third, your form is the place to look for the answers to

Flex Wheeler

your troubles. If none of these questions applies to you, you are ahead of the game and should grow like a weed from this routine. The rest of you must perfect your form first – *then* grow like a weed! Of course, your genetics have the final say as to how much muscle you can build, but don't think for a minute you can't add new muscle to your back following this routine and these training tips.

Never heave or swing your weights. Whether you are doing a cable row, bent row or lat pulldown, keep a constant tension on the muscle at all times. When you are doing any type of rowing movement, your back should be in a fixed position. There should be no swaying back and forth or up and down. When you are using exceptionally heavy weight, there will be some movement of the upper body, but it should not be too exaggerated. It should be the natural rhythm of the movement, and not some heavefest to impress your buddies or the opposite sex. Pick a weight with which you can keep the torso relatively stable, and use the lats to do the work, not the lower back and biceps. "But what about the stretch?" some people might ask. The stretch is very important, but it should come from the lats and muscles of the upper back, and it does not require you to lean all the way forward. If you keep the torso stable and let the lats do the stretching, you will get the intended benefit of the stretch.

When doing any back movement such as chinups, pulldowns or cable rows, stick your chest out, arch your back slightly and squeeze the shoulder blades together as hard as you can while pulling the arms and shoulders as far back or down (depending on the movement) as possible. Using strict form could make all your weights go down, but the pay-off will be watching your muscle mass go up. If you can check the ego at the door, you could find one day that you have difficulty getting through the doorway because of the size of your back!

The Paradox of Back-Training

Back-training can be something of a paradox. Why, you ask? The back, being as large and complex as it is, presents a special problem for many bodybuilders. To hit all the areas of the back sufficiently, you need to do power exercises such as deadlifts, exercises for width such as chinups and pulldowns, and exercises for thickness and density such as bent rows and cable rows. Herein lies the conundrum. Try to do all these exercises in the same workout, and burnout (i.e. severe overtraining) is sure to follow. If you do two exercises for power, two or three exercises for width, and two or three exercises for thickness, you will be doing far more sets than you could ever hope to recuperate from, and the workout will last far too long to be productive. Yet, if you avoid doing all of the exercises, or do only one of each, a flat small back could be the result. You see it all the time in the gym. A person will have great back thickness but no width, or great width but no thickness, or good width and thickness through the upper back but no muscle in the lower region. This defect is caused by a disproportionate dependence on one type of back exercise while avoiding others.

What to do? By splitting up the back into three separate workouts that emphasize the various needs of this particular muscle group, you can have the best of both worlds and be able to do all the exercises you need

Dorian Yates

without overtraining. Schedule (1) a power workout for the lower back and overall back strength, (2) a thickness and density workout, and (3) a width workout. You will properly hit all the areas of the back with sufficient exercises in a short enough time frame to avoid overtraining and still stimulate this complex muscle group. This strategy has worked wonders for the bodybuilders I have trained who had uneven back development, or had stopped making gains in that bodypart. It has definitely helped me too, though I am certainly no Lee Haney in the back department.

Getting Down To Business (i.e. Doing the Nasty)

Workout #1, the anabolic power workout:
(1) partial-rep deadlifts in the power cage.

Set the pins in the power cage to just below the knee caps. You will do 6 sets of this exercise. Starting with higher reps (10-12) for the first set or two, work your way down, using progressively heavier weights, to a set or two of 3 to 5 reps with the heaviest weight possible. Try to pull with your whole back, not just your traps, lower back and biceps. Concentrate on flexing the lats during the movement, and you will be surprised how good a pump you can get. This technique takes some mental concentration and time, but once you get the hang of it, it really does work.

Start

Mike O'Hearn pulls a heavy deadlift at Gold's Gym/ Venice. *Finish*

2) regular deadlifts off the floor.

You will do 3 sets of these. Take approximately 50 percent of the weight you did 3 to 5 reps with in the cage, and do (or at least try to do) 3 sets of 12-15 reps of regular deadlifts off the floor... and don't expect to do much in the way of exercise the next day!

Tony Pearson performs lat pulldown to the rear. *Finish*

Start

Denise Rutkowski

Workout #2, thickness and density:
(1) Bent rows, 4 x 6 - 8 reps
(2) Cables rows, 3 x 8 - 10 reps
(3) T-bar rows, 3 x 10 - 12 reps
(4) Chinups, one set until failure to finish with a great pump. (Note: When doing chinups, you should lean back and pull up to your sternum. Arch your back and squeeze your shoulder blades together at the top.)

Workout #3, width:
(1) Wide-grip chinups to the front (see form tip above), 4 x 8 - 12 reps
(2) Wide-grip pulldowns behind the neck 3 x 10 - 12 reps
(3) Close-grip (or reverse-grip) pulldowns, 3 x 10 - 12 reps
(4) Partial-rep deadlifts in the cage, 1 x 12 - 15 reps

(Note: Remember to flex the lats. Thrust chest forward, pull shoulder blades back, and squeeze the lats hard at the top of each rep.)

Conclusion
Making It Work
For You

Using this format for back-training, you will be able to focus on each area of the back with enough sets and exercises, in a minimum amount of time, to cause the growth you desire while dramatically reducing the potential for overtraining. Of course, you could still be in an overtrained state if you are in the gym too often, not eating enough calories and protein, and/or not getting enough sleep. Your best bet would be to do one back workout per week. For example, you could do #l on Monday, #2 the following Monday, and #3 seven days after that. Then repeat the cycle. You don't have to do it exactly that way, but I would give at least five to seven days between back workouts no matter how you break it up. Pull that weight belt tight, put your straps on, and start saving your money now for larger clothing!

Kevin Levrone and Dorian Yates match back double-biceps poses.

Chapter Twelve

Who Really Wants Great Legs?

Gary Strydom

The title of this chapter poses a serious question to you. Do you really want to grow great legs? Sure, people say they do, but when leg day rolls around the excuses fly fast and furious – excuses such as "My favorite squat rack is taken... let's bag legs for today" or "I forgot to bring my water bottle with me... let's do biceps instead." I am sure you can come up with a few more. Many a bodybuilder and bodybuilding writer (especially me) has suggested that the only thing more painful than a serious calf workout is a set of high-rep squats. 'Oh man,' you're thinking, 'did he just say high-rep squats?' You bet your ass I did. Unless you have a whole closet full of baggies, so no one ever sees you in a pair of shorts or spandex, it could be time to get serious about leg-training. Hey, if you already have great legs, the kind that look good from every angle, the kind that create jealous stares in the gym, send me a picture. If you don't, this could be the chapter for you.

One myth in bodybuilding that really needs to die here and now is this: "Low reps build muscle and high reps define and shape the muscle." In truth, a combination of both high- and low-rep schemes is the best way to grow serious muscle tissue (see chapters 3 and 10), especially when trying to kick-start those stubborn quadriceps, or any bodypart for that matter. With some rare exceptions, this strategy seldom fails to work. Another bad habit people have is equating high reps with light weight and low reps with heavy weight. Who ever said you should use light weights because you are doing high reps? You should endeavor to use as much weight as humanly possible for whatever number of reps you have chosen. After your first few years of training (when you have developed a good base) legs generally grow best from moderate to high reps anyway. Heavy-weight/high-rep sets can be the most productive sets you will ever experience. They are also the most painful, as you will find out if you follow the leg routines that are outlined in this chapter. Without excep-

Leg-training is what separates the men from the boys.

tion these routines and training tips always add inches to the most stubborn legs.

Remember that "heavy" is a relative term. If you spread your legs wide and stick your butt out when you squat, you will be able to use more weight than if you had a narrow stance and didn't stick your butt out. The question is, would your thighs be working harder with the powerlifting stance (i.e. wide stance) and extra weight? The answer is a resounding no! In the wide stance the muscles of your lower back (erectors), hips and glutes are far more involved than your thighs. The narrow stance would be best if your goal is swept-out, shaped-out and awesome thighs, while possibly avoiding the big butt, wide hips and large obliques that often result from the wide-footed squatting stance.

Size for the sake of size is useless. A guy with 25-inch thighs that sweep off the knee and taper into the hip, who has equal-sized hamstrings to boot, will always look more impressive than a guy with 30-inch thighs that are blocky and shapeless. You can't take a tape measure onstage at a contest, and you can't take it to the beach (unless you're a complete zipper-head). Of course, the best of both worlds is a thigh that is both big and shaped out. Though the absolute

muscle size and shape you can achieve is genetically predetermined, you will be amazed how much you can change the shape of your legs (or any bodypart) if you train for it. So I ask you again, do you wanna grow some legs? If the answer is yes, as I hope it is, read on.

The Warmup

Before we can even begin to discuss serious leg-training, we have to consider the importance of the warmup. "I warm up," some people might say. "I do one set of squats with 135 for a warmup." That's not a warmup – that's an injury waiting to happen. A proper warmup will make you stronger, far less likely to suffer an injury, and has the net benefit of making you grow faster. A proper warmup will allow you to climb faster to your heaviest weight, so you will not have to waste time on useless sets which drain you of your energy both mentally and physically. Because these leg routines are low in sets and high in intensity, they are completely dependent on the correct utilization of the warmup. In short, if you're too lazy to do the warmup, don't bother to do the workouts. If you skip the warmup, don't blame me when your knees sound like two pieces of sandpaper rubbing together.

As an added bonus, I have seen the nagging injuries of hundreds of bodybuilders completely disappear by just showing them a proper warmup for the affected area. Here is the warmup you should do before each of the three workouts: First, ride the stationary bike for five minutes. Second, do 2 sets of 15 reps on the leg extension with a very light weight (40 - 60 pounds). Third, do 2 sets of squats with only the bar for 15 reps. Fourth and last, do some light stretching. Now you're ready to rock 'n' roll! Unfortunately for the people who don't like serious leg workouts, they will be unable to use light weight for countless sets because they are "warming up!"

Start

Stretching

Stretching is invaluable for growing great legs. All bodyparts respond well to stretching, but for some unknown reason (at least to me anyway) the muscles of the legs respond the most dramatically. Stretching a muscle lengthens it and gives it more room to grow. A long, full muscle always looks better than a bunched-up one. Think about it. Most of the greatest legs belong(ed) to men who are extremely flexible. Tom Platz, Flex Wheeler and Phil Hill come quickly to mind. Notice I didn't say the biggest, but the *greatest*. Which would you rather be known for? More than anything else you can do, stretching can alter the shape of your legs to that desired "swept" look. I have seen the transformation dozens of times, and it never ceases to amaze me. Stretching also has the added benefit, as does a proper warmup, of reducing your chance of injuries, which are certainly not conducive to growth. You can blow it off, or benefit from it like the pros. I have always considered proper stretching to be one of the "secrets" of the pros that most people don't utilize to their advantage. You should do light stretching before the workout and the serious stretching afterward.

Finish

One of the finest exercises for overall mass-building is the deep squat. – Bob Cicherillo

Workout #I : Just Squat!

These three workouts are in sequence. If you are a beginner, stop right here because this is all you will need for another year or so. If you are an intermediate or advanced body-builder, you have the misfortune of being able to do the next two workouts. The two most important sets in this workout are the last two. They should be absolute maximal efforts. The high-rep set should be at least 60 to 70 percent as heavy as the last low-rep set. For example, if you can squat 350 pounds for 6 to 8 reps, you should be able to squat 225 pounds (225 is approximately 65 percent of 350) for 20 to 25 reps. Have a garbage can close by – you might need it! This workout may look deceivingly simple, but if you put the correct amount of intensity into it, you should be looking for a stretcher, not another machine to get onto. Try constantly to increase the weight of the last two sets. If you add five pounds to the low-rep set, you should be able to add five pounds to the high-rep set. This is the squat rep scheme to follow after the warmup:

Kevin Levrone, Dorian Yates and Nasser El Sonbaty at the Mr. Olympia contest.

Set #1:
1 x 10 - 12 reps
Set #2:
I x 10 reps
Set #3:
I x 8 - 10 reps
Sets #4 and 5:
2 x 6 - 8 reps
Set #6:
I x 20 - 25 reps.

Tips and pointers for workout #I

Many people have a great deal of difficulty squatting. Besides the fact that squats leave you feeling as if a train just ran you over, maintaining correct form during the movement can be hard. This problem is due to several reasons. The most common is an inflexibility in either the ankles or hips (or both). This lack of flexibility is usually compounded by a weak midsection which makes the person lean too far forward, thus pretty much nullifying the benefit of the exercise and primarily working the glutes, hips and erectors. If you are one of these people, with a little work you can dramatically improve your squat form. This brings us back to stretching. If you work hard at increasing your flexibility

Start

Finish

in the ankles and hips you will be able to stay more upright when squatting.

    As for the midsection weakness, I learned this by accident a few years ago. After talking with a few professional bodybuilders about their back-training (I know this is the chapter about leg-training, but bear with me), I was advised to rely exclusively on rowing movements instead of chinups, pulldowns, etc. if I was having trouble developing my back, as I was. (Their advice later developed into the routines in chap 11.) Besides acquiring a better back, I noticed my form in the squat greatly improved as a result of the increased erector strength and overall back development. Boy, was I happy! From that day on every bodybuilder I gave the same advice to concerning squatting troubles noticed an improvement in his form. This approach takes a few months or more to work, but it's worth the effort. I know this sounds weird, but try the back routines #l and #2 from chapter 11

Paul "Quadzilla" DeMayo burns his quads on the leg-extension machine.

exclusively for a few months if you want to improve your squat form and your back development. A quick tip before we move on: Make sure you leave at least a few days between your leg day and your back day, or your lower back will be too fried to move a pencil!

Workout #2: Size and Shape

    This workout is meant to really focus in on leg development and shape. It is almost as hard as the third workout. You will notice that I have put leg extensions first. Leg extensions are the most underrated thigh exercise in existence. This exercise allows you to completely isolate the thighs without using the hips, back or glutes. Contrary to popular belief, leg extensions work the entire thigh, not just the vastus (tear drop). They will allow you to pre-exhaust your thighs, so they will be additionally stimulated during subsequent exercises, and will reduce the involvement of the glutes, hips and back. What else could you ask for from an exercise? A serious mistake that many bodybuilders make is that they don't put enough effort into their leg extensions. It is not an uncommon sight to witness some strong-ass bodybuilder squat with 700 pounds for reps, then go do leg extensions with 100 pounds when he should be using the entire stack. Take this exercise seriously, and you will have the last laugh. Remember, you should have done the warmup I outlined above, so almost every set of this workout ought to be an all-out effort. It looks like this:

(1) Leg extensions, 3 x l0 - 12 reps
(2) Smith-machine squats, 4 x l0 - 12 reps
(3) Hack squats, 3 x l0 - 12 reps
(4) Leg curls, 4 x l0 - 12 reps

Tips and pointers for workout #2

An oversight of many bodybuilders is a lack of emphasis on the eccentric (negative) part of the movement. The eccentric part of any exercise is mainly responsible for the cellular disruption that leads to remodeling (growth) of muscle tissue. You can see this mistake happening in the gym all the time. A person will let the leg sled drop without control, then press it back up, or he will descend quickly into the squat or drop the leg extension without control. Big mistake! This bad form indicates a lack of concentration or the use of too much weight, and generally sucks for building quality muscle. You should concentrate on building muscle. Leave the ego-building to someone else. When doing your Smith squats, don't walk your feet out far in front of you. This position is the same as for a power squat, and it over-emphasizes the hips, back and glutes. Your feet should be just slightly in front of you and the stance narrower than your shoulders. You should descend all the way down into the squat – far below parallel. Inability to do this is a sign that you are not flexible enough (see stretching above).

Bob Cicherillo blasts his quads on the leg press.

Tom Platz flexes his mighty quads.

Workout #3: Simple, But Oh So Painful

This workout can cause a pump that will border on the bizarre. Remember, just because you see it calls for high reps does not give you an excuse to use wussy weights. You will be surprised at how much weight you can use if you put your mind to it.

(1) Leg extensions, 3 x 20 reps.
(2) Leg presses or Smith squats, 3 x 15 - 20 reps.
(3) Lunge walks*, 3 cycles
(4) Leg curls, 3 x 15 reps.
(5) Straight-leg deadlifts, 2 x 15 reps.

(*) If you have never done lunge walks, you are in for a most unpleasant experience, but man, are they great for improving leg shape! This exercise is similar to a regular lunge except that you actually lunge across the floor instead of staying in place. If you take a dumbell in each hand and step out far into a lunge, you will be in the normal lunge position. Instead of standing back up, you will pull your back foot through to take another step forward. Basically you are just walking across the gym floor (looking fairly goofy) while taking extremely large steps. Make sure you descend all the way into the lunge on every step. Your back kneecap should just brush the ground when you descend, indicating you have gone down far enough. Most people move some benches out of the way so they can get about 30 or more feet of walking space. Lunge-walk the 30 feet (or about 10 steps), turn around and come back. This would count as one cycle of this exercise. You could also use a long hallway.

Tips and pointers for workout #3
Hold onto your cookies – it's a real killer!

Conclusion

No one will blame you if you turn the page and pass over these routines for leg growth. You won't be the first person to avoid them. If you do decide to try these three workouts, I would recommend doing each workout once a week (in the three-day-per-week or four-day-per-week workout schedule mentioned in the introduction of this book) if you are looking to get the most benefit without overtraining.

A contest-ready
Paul DeMayo

Chapter Thirteen

There's More Than One Way To Build A Chest

Into each life a little rain must fall, but people who can't make any headway on their chest development feel as if it's raining all the time. The chest is probably the most individualized of all bodyparts. It can also be one of the most frustrating. Though there seems to be a general consensus on how to train most major areas of the body – such as back, legs and shoulders – ask ten different bodybuilders how they work their chest and you will get ten different answers. Sure, there are differences of opinion on every bodypart, but nowhere do the opinions vary as much as for the pectorals. To bench press or not to bench press, low reps or high reps, to pre-exhaust or not to pre-exhaust...the list is long and it occasionally causes people to throw their muscle magazine across the room in irritation. I know. I have done it!

On the positive side the chest is a bodypart that responds quickly once you have found the formula that works for you. This chapter is going to dissect some of these topics, separate the wheat from the chaff so to speak, so that you can make an informed decision on how to put together your own personalized chest routine and get those stubborn protuberances growing.

Chris Cormier

To Bench Or Not To Bench

This is an argument that goes back and forth among bodybuilders all the time. Certain people, because of biomechanical and structural advantages, derive great benefit from flat benching. The benefit does not seem to be related, though, to how strong the person is at this movement. Some people are what you could call "delt/triceps pushers." They can be extremely strong at bench pressing without involving the muscles of their chest to any great degree. Their pecs act as more of a stabilizer while their delts and triceps do most of the pushing. This style might be fine for a powerlifter, but it is a real detriment for the bodybuilder.

A close friend of mine could bench press 535 pounds in strict form by the time he was nineteen years old. Believe it or not, his chest was his visually weakest bodypart! He did, however, have the largest shoulders and triceps I have ever seen. Though he did not give up bench pressing, he started concentrating more on flyes and other movements that isolate the pectorals. Within a short time his chest matched the rest of his body. Conversely, you will see people who work with relatively light weights when benching, but whose pecs swell up like balloons during each rep. The reason could be their bone structure. It could be the way their tendons attach to their bones, combined with the number of muscle cells they have in that particular area. It is most likely a combination of all three factors.

If you are a beginner, bench pressing is definitely for you. Only after several years of training will you know whether it is a productive movement or not. Certainly it is a good, solid, multijoint exercise for the beginner. If you have been benching for a few years and all you feel on bench day is dread followed by sore delts and triceps the next morning, you might be advised to give it up. Some people are just not biomechanically set up for flat bench pressing. Make no mistake about it – you can still develop great pecs. You might, as so many people have, find other pressing movements – such as incline Smith-machine benching, upright bench machine and flat dumbell presses – to be more effective.

Before you drop flat benching, it would be worth your while to reassess your form on this exercise. There have been many good articles in the various muscle mags on how to improve your form on the bench press. I suggest you look through back issues of your favorite magazines if you have your heart set on benching, though the bench press is not my favorite exercise for the intermediate to advanced bodybuilder aiming to build world-class pecs. Also I believe the injury potential of flat bench pressing is greater than its benefit to the muscles of the chest. I have seen more bodybuilding careers ended by pec injuries from flat bench pressing than by problems resulting from any other exercise.

Vince Taylor

One last comment should be made about benching before I close out this section: Don't let your ego get the best of you. Don't feel you are less of a bodybuilder if you don't bench press until your hair falls out. The most successful bodybuilders in the world know how to check their ego at the door and do what is right for them, not what will impress the gym rats.

A good all-pressing routine you might try would include the following exercises:
(1) Wide incline Smith bench
(2) Flat dumbell press
(3) Upright bench machine

Pre-exhausting

Here is a gem of a technique too many bodybuilders ignore. Most bodyparts respond well to pre-exhausting, especially the chest. "Delt/triceps pushers" will get particularly good results from this system. Pre-exhausting involves doing an isolation movement such as flyes before a compound movement like the upright bench machine. This sequence allows you to isolate your chest early in the workout, thus pre-exhausting the pecs and making them work harder during the subsequent pressing exercises. I have found this technique works especially well for people trying to improve their upper pec development, the area of the chest most often lacking in beginning and intermediate body-builders. You can do it every time you train chest, or alternate it every other workout. Give the pre-exhaust system a try for a few months and you will definitely notice some new growth and improved shape. A good pre-exhaust chest routine could look like this:

(1) Incline flyes, flat flyes or cable crossovers
(2) Wide incline Smith-machine benches
(3) Flat dumbell presses
(4) Weighted dips

Laura
Creavalle

High Reps vs. Low Reps

Some people, because of the leverage factors I have already mentioned, are able to use huge poundages for low reps and still get a good pump. This ability has a tendency to make everyone else who is watching these strong individuals feel needlessly compelled to do the same. A good pump does not necessarily mean that muscle growth is taking place, but it is a reliable indicator that the muscle you are intending to work is actually being used. I could go into a long detailed discussion about the different types of muscle fiber and how they react to various rep ranges, but there is no need. Body-builders have never paid much attention to this information anyway because they know that what looks good in a textbook does not always transfer into the gym.

If you are unable to feel your chest working at the lower rep ranges, and you fail to get a pump or any soreness in your chest the following day, experiment with different rep schemes to find what works for you. I wish there were a blanket answer to the best number of reps that would make your pecs grow, but this is where you need to do some of your own research. Remember that many great chests have been built on moderate to high reps. Don't feel you have to put a Chevy Malibu on each end of the bar to make your pecs grow. Just be sure that you are controlling the weight and not the other way around. This does not mean using "light" weights for high reps. You should try to use as much weight as possible for whatever number of reps you have chosen.

A beginner should endeavor to get as strong as possible on all the basic movements (see chapter 3) such as the bench press, squat and bent-over row, using moderately low reps. After a few years of training, some people will find they react more favorably to different rep ranges, while others will continue to get larger and stronger using low reps. You will also discover as time goes by that different bodyparts need different rep strategies to grow. For instance, your back might grow best on 8 to 10 reps, chest on 10 to 12, legs on 12 to 15 and so

Start

Finish

Ultramassive Lee Priest performs incline dumbell flyes at Gold's Gym/Venice. Productive chest-training is a highly individualized matter.

on. So don't think because your legs have been growing fine on a particular rep scheme that your chest will also. You can either alternate high-rep days with low-rep days (a popular approach with many bodybuilders) or incorporate different reps in the same workout (see

chapters 3 and 10). A low-rep/high-rep alternating chest workout could be structured like this:

Workout #I (low-rep):
(1) Upright bench machine, 6 - 8 reps
(2) Incline dumbell presses, 8 -10 reps
(3) Weighted dips, 8 - 10 reps
(4) Cross-bench pullovers, 12 - 15 reps

Workout #2 (high-rep):
(1) Incline flyes, 10 - 12 reps
(2) "High-neck" incline Smith-machine benches, 10 - 12 reps
(3) Cable crossovers, 12 - 15+ reps
(4) Dips (bodyweight only), 15+ reps

A routine that integrates varying reps in the same workout might look like this:
(1) Flat dumbell presses, 6 - 8 reps per set
(2) Incline Smith benches, 8 - 10 reps per set
(3) Weighted dips, 10 - 12 reps per set
(4) Flat flyes, 12 - 15+ reps per set

I suggest that beginners should do 6 to 8 sets for chest, intermediates 8 to 10, and advanced intermediate 10 to 12 sets. These figures are not carved in stone however, as some of the most massive bodybuilders in history have used many fewer sets or many more. Dorian Yates, David Dearth and Mike Mentzer prefer

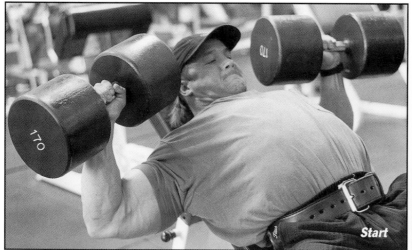

Start   Finish

Using the power of Hercules, Craig Titus drives up 170-pound dumbells on the incline press.

very few sets for chest (and other bodyparts). Arnold you-only-need-to-see-his-first-name, Milos Sarcev and Sonny Schmidt prefer more. Don't be afraid to experiment (see chapters 3 and 10 for more info). Why do you think there is such a dramatic difference in the number

Start

Tom Pattyn performs cable crossovers. Finish

of sets these champions do for their chest? Years of experimentation to find out what works for them – that's why. Don't follow the pack, or you end up looking like the pack!

Another good rule of thumb is, don't train your chest like a major bodypart until it is one. As with any muscle, in your zeal to grow, you can easily overtrain and get injured, sick or just burned out. Obviously none of these conditions is conducive to growth.

As for my personal opinion on the matter of how many sets a person should do, it should be obvious to the reader by this point in the book that I am a firm believer in using low to moderate sets – with maximum intensity! – if maximum size is the goal. As Lee Haney always says, "Stimulate, don't annihilate." At the risk of repeating myself from past chapters and various articles, don't think you can skip breakfast, have a weight-gain drink for lunch and a small dinner and make any gains in a stubborn bodypart because it ain't gonna happen. Eat four to six squares a day, plus the correct supplements and other nutrients discussed throughout this book (see chapters 3, 4, and 10), and you will be in business. Design your own chest routine based on your needs and what level you are at as a bodybuilder, not on your ego or what other people are doing around you. If you take one part brains and two parts hard work and apply the mix to what you have read here, your chest could make new stretch marks in your T-shirts!

The striations on Lee Priest's chest confirm that the man is ripped!

Chapter Fourteen
Turning Calves Into Cows

F#@%, what a burn! That's all that can be said when a serious calf workout is finally over. You shouldn't count sets when you do calves. You will know it is over when a walk to the water fountain is no longer possible. But seriously, besides a high-rep squat workout (see chapter 12), high-intensity calf-training is

Vince Taylor

probably the most uncomfortable and down-right painful workout around. Very few people are willing to put up with the discomfort of a proper calf workout to get a good set of calves. Actually, the majority have convinced themselves that unless you are born with good calves you will never have any. Of course, that's because their calves didn't explode into some sort of Mike Matarazzo/Jeff King hybrid after a few months of training them. They throw up their hands in disgust, throw in a few sets for calves at the end of a workout, and mutter, "He was born with them" at anyone with a good pair.

I am reminded of a conversation I had in the gym some time ago with a friend of mine who shall remain nameless (and probably calf-less). After finishing a set of standing calf raises, he exclaimed, "I have tried everything for them, and they don't grow!" To which I replied, "Have you tried hard work?" Though clearly put out by my comment, he went on to tell me that he had really blasted them for a few months and nothing really happened. "Besides," he mumbled, "what do you know about stubborn calves, having obviously been born with good calves?" "Ha!" I retorted, and quickly pointed out to him how wrong he was. I explained that I had started with calves that measured under 13 inches, and that only after years – not months – of painful, leg-numbing, torturous calf workouts did I get them up to their current measurement of 17 inches. Granted, a 17-inch calf is not a huge calf, but considering where they started, and that my ankles measure only seven inches, they are respectable. Yes, this chapter is here to tell you that you can build a respectable pair of calves even if you were not born with them. I can honestly say that every person who has been forced (usually screaming and kicking) to do these calf routines on a regular basis for at least six months has added new size to his lower appendages.

Of course, there are those people whom God decided to bless with great calves (we hate

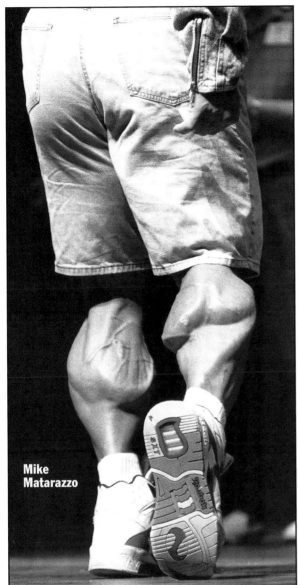

Mike Matarazzo

Consistency + Intensity = Results

Consistency and intensity are important for every bodypart, but no bodypart is as dependent on these two variables as calves, especially if, like most of us, you have average genetics in the lower-leg department. Because of the type of muscle fiber and that particular type of pain they are able to emit, calves take a physical effort and mental stamina that goes beyond what is required by almost any other bodypart, so you had better be ready for some hard work. They should be given their own time, not be trained as an afterthought. How will you know if you are consistent enough? Don't miss a scheduled calf workout, period. How do you figure intensity? Count only the reps that burn. If the burn starts on the eighth rep, then the ninth rep would actually be rep number one, and so on. Intensity is a hard concept to explain on paper, but this technique really helps to raise the intensity level of calf workouts. You want to shoot for 15 to 20 reps, not including the ones that didn't burn.

Standing calf raises are a great lower-leg builder.
Start   **Finish**

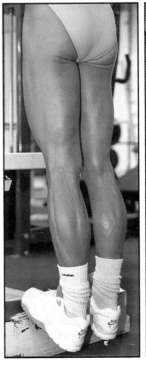

those people), and yes, there are people who just can't get them. But there are only a few in the first group, and not as many as you think in the second. I have personally taken people with small calves and put size on them. They didn't like me very much afterward, but that's another story. These are some workouts and training tips that have worked consistently for the bodybuilders that I train. I won't blame you if, after doing these workouts, you quit because you are too sore to walk up the stairs to work the next day. If you stick to these workouts religiously, however, your calves will have only two choices: They will either grow or fall off!

Foot Position and Rep Speed

Your stance should be a little narrower than shoulder width with knees just slightly bent. The most important facts to know about foot position are these: Your feet should be slightly pigeon toed (heels wider than toes), and you should try to keep all the pressure over the big toe. If you look closely at people doing calves, you'll notice that they tend to roll their feet outward, taking the pressure off the muscle. This style robs them of the full contraction. Keeping the pressure over the big toe, or at least trying to, will eliminate this problem. This might seem trivial, but believe me, it is the key to successfully working your calves. All too often you will see someone with a huge amount of weight bouncing up and down on a calf machine. All this does is put a lot of stress on the tendons and ligaments of the foot and calf while doing very little for the muscle. Use as much weight as you can while keeping the reps smooth and slow. You should get a full stretch and a full contraction, which you will really feel if you follow the tips for foot placement.

The schedule goes like this: You choose one of the three calf workouts outlined below, which you will alternate on a separate day with 4 sets of standing calf raises and 4 sets of seated calf raises. Wait five to seven days between calf workouts, or until walking becomes normal again! A good schedule could be as follows: Monday do workout #1; Friday do 4 sets of standing calf raises and 4 sets of seated calf raises. The following Monday pick another one of the three workouts, and so on. It is best to alternate these workouts with the easier day so that the muscle can fully recuperate.

Before we get to the workouts, we need to go over some terminology so that there will be no confusion when you see it in the exercise outlines. You will be utilizing all of the training principles outlined below. Some people consider a drop set and descending sets as the same method, but I have separated them into two different techniques.

Lisa Lorio can't resist feeling Roger Stewart's incredible calves.

• **Drop sets:** Working a muscle until failure, then immediately lowering the weight and continuing the set until failure occurs again. This can be done three or four times in a single set (very painful).

• **Descending sets:** Starting the first set with the heaviest weight you can use, then lowering weight each succeeding set (brings tears to your eyes). Should be done only after a full warmup.

• **100-rep pump:** After finishing a regular set of calves on a machine, immediately go over to a calf block and do 100 slow reps (a real burn-o-rama).

• **60-rep system:** While using a standing calf machine, place feet as wide as you can on machine platform and do 20 strict reps. Remaining on the machine, quickly stretch out calves, move them inward to about shoulder width, do another 20 strict reps and stretch again. For the final 20 reps put feet together so that they are touching, and complete the set. (Calves will be too numb to burn.)

• **Partials:** After going to failure with perfectly strict reps, stay on machine and complete an additional 12 to 15 reps, using only half the range of motion. When doing partials on a seated calf machine, assuming you have done 15 to 20 strict reps, lean forward, place your elbows on the pads, and press down with the full weight of your upper body. Now complete your partial reps. (Falling on floor and holding calves not unusual.)

Machine donkey calf raises as performed by Roger Stewart. *Finish*

Start

Full stretch and contraction are necessary in calf-training for maximum results.

The Workouts

Workout #1:
Do 3 supersets of standing calf raises, seated calf raises and 100-rep pump. You should take no rest between these exercises. The 3 supersets will be a total of 9 sets for calves.

Workout #2:
(1) Calf raises on 45-degree leg press with a drop set on the last set. Have a partner strip plates for you (4 sets).
(2) Seated calf raises with partials on the last set (3-4 sets).
(3) Standing calf raises using 60-rep system on last set (3-4 sets).

Workout #3
(1) Standing calf raises using descending sets (4 sets).
(2) Seated calf raises with partials on last two sets (3-4 sets).
(3) Donkey calf raises with a drop set on final set (3-4 sets).

So what's the payoff for all this hard work? You might be aware of this already, but if you're not you should be. There is not a more impressive sight in all of bodybuilding than a really well-developed set of calves. It completely separates the serious bodybuilder from the wannabes. A well-developed set of calves will be immediately noticed and appreciated – for the obvious hard work you have put into them – by both the general public and, most importantly, the bodybuilding community (who are a hard bunch to impress). Great calves are the rarest sight you will see, and the hardest muscles to obtain, which makes them the bodypart most often responsible for a person winning or losing a trophy. I have always strived to be one of those writers who don't tell you what you want to hear, but rather what you need to hear. I hope I have continued this trend by telling you everything I think you need to know about calf-training. Hey, if you're happy with your calf development, that's great. If you're not, give these workouts all you can and watch those bad boys grow.

A good set of calves always draws attention. – Lee Priest

Chapter Fifteen
Armed and Dangerous

There is nothing in all of bodybuilding that personifies the sport more than a pair of big "guns." Huge arms are always the first visual attraction to draw most young men (or women) to the sport in the first place. People are often bitten by "the bug" after seeing a picture of some famous bodybuilder's huge, peaked cannons jumping out at them from the glossy cover of a muscle magazine. If you asked the majority of successful competitors what started them on the road to muscledom, they would invariably say something like, "I saw Arnold on the cover of a magazine doing a double-biceps shot and I knew right there and then I wanted to look like that." Judges and bodybuilding aficionados tend to look at overall balance and symmetry of an athlete when judging a physique (as they should), but to the average guy or girl who grinds out each set at the local gym, the arms are where it's at when it comes to impressive body-parts to strive for.

Ronnie Coleman's arms are truly impressive.

I have stated several times in my articles for *MuscleMag International* that building impressive arms is a fairly straightforward endeavor, and people tend to make too big a deal about it. Then I got those letters. What letters, you say? The half-dozen or so I received in my post-office box that said, "Hey, Brink, if building arms is so damned easy, why am I having such a tough time of it?" or "If you tell me one more time that building arms is easy, I will be forced to break one of yours!" OK, OK, so maybe building big arms is not so easy for everyone after all. I sat down and put on my thinking cap, the one that says "dunce" on the front of it from fifth grade. I got down to business trying to devise a routine that would add arm size to the most stubborn Pee-Wee Herman-sized arm, and damned if I didn't come up with one.

It had to be based on the most effective exercises for building biceps and triceps. It had to keep boredom and the dreaded training rut away. Most of all, it had to prevent overtraining of these small muscle groups. In short, it had to combine all the factors I know about – exercise choice, rep ranges, etc. – that can bring about renewed growth in the arms of hard gainers. If you are one of these people, or one of those guys who sent me a nasty letter, this is the routine for you.

Picking the Right Exercises and Avoiding Overtraining

Without a doubt overtraining and the wrong choice of exercises are the two major factors (genetics notwithstanding) between arms of string and arms that stretch out the sleeves of a T-shirt. After a tough back day your biceps can range from slightly stiff to downright sore as hell. After a killer chest day sore triceps are more than common. It does not take the deductive reasoning power of a Sherlock Holmes to figure out that chest-training and back-training (also delt-training) directly stress the biceps and triceps.

Look at it this way: If you do 15 sets for chest, then go on to do 12 sets for triceps, that's a total of 27 sets for triceps! The same holds true for the back/biceps relationship. Obviously there is no way a small muscle group like biceps or triceps will be able to recuperate, much less grow, from that many sets, yet that is exactly what most people do. For the genetically gifted and/or chemically assisted, this is not as much a problem, but for the hard gainer overtraining is an arm-growing disaster. The low sets of this routine, and the scheduled break (I call it a "nonworkout"), will alleviate this problem. I know you will be tempted to skip over the break period or add extra sets, but that will only guarantee the failure of this arm-training program. Check the ego at the door and watch your arms grow.

Debbie Muggli

Overcoming the Boredom Factor

To put sheer mass on the muscles of the upper arm, there are only a few exercises the hard gainer will find truly effective. For biceps the straight-bar curl (the granddaddy of mass-builders) and seated incline dumbell curl are the two that work best. For triceps, it is the close-grip bench press and incline lying triceps extension. Generally speaking, arm-training should be based on these exercises if mass is your goal. I think most people instinctively know these exercises stimulate the most muscle, but

Darin Lannaghan

the boredom factor sets in and before they know it they are doing specialized exercises such as one-arm cable kickbacks and concentration curls and getting nowhere fast. Don't get me wrong. Concentration curls and triceps kickbacks have their place as shaping movements for trainers who have already developed good size in their arms, but you can't shape something you don't have, so leave these exercises to the people who have no complaints about size.

By making minor changes in form and rep range, and adding in a scheduled break at key points, you can avoid the boredom factor and the potential for overtraining. Many body-builders have made good gains on exercises such as preacher curls and triceps pushdowns, and these can be included occasionally, but the previously mentioned exercises – straight-bar curls, close-grip bench presses, etc. – are notoriously effective for people having a tough time making headway with their arm development. Of course, if you're severely overtraining your arms (or any bodypart), it does not really matter what exercises you pick, and this is a very important consideration to keep in mind.

Workout #I: Heavy and Basic
Biceps:
(1) Straight-bar curls, 3 x 6-10 reps
Form: Use a grip slightly narrower than shoulder width. Shoot for 6 to 10 reps. You can cheat (i.e. employ a slight swaying of the upper body) on the last few reps of a set, but if you have to cheat at anything under 6 reps, the weight is too heavy. Don't waste your time by attempting

Lee Priest caught on film performing heavy barbell curls. *Start*

to heave up huge weights in bad form. Doing this only transfers the stress to your lower back, traps and delts. It might look cool to the average person, but it's a fast way to sabotage your biceps growth.

(2) Incline seated dumbell curls, 3 x 8-10 reps

Form: Set an upright bench to about 75 or 80 degrees. Use a weight you can get at least 8 strict reps with. Cheat up 1 or 2 reps at the end of the set.

Triceps:

(1) Close-grip bench presses, 3 x 6-10 reps

Form: Lie on a flat bench in the normal position for bench pressing (i.e. feet on floor wider than shoulders and back slightly arched). Take a grip with hands about 10 to 12 inches apart and bring weight down to about the nipple line. Do not bounce the weight off your chest! If you can't do the reps smoothly, you're using too much weight. A few forced reps, after completing 6 to 8 strict reps, is fine to do for a little added triceps stimulation.

(2) Incline triceps extensions, 3 x 8-10 reps

Form: This exercise is similar to normal lying triceps extensions except that you set the bench at a slight angle – about 30-40 degrees. A slight angle during lying extensions allows for a better stretch, better contraction and less elbow stress, which is common with this exercise.

Workout #2: High Reps and a Change in Form

Triceps:

(1) Close-grip bench presses, 3 x 12-15 reps. This time you start the workout with triceps and use a slightly different form for this exercise.

Form: Lie on flat bench and put feet up on bench. Take the same grip as before but bring the bar down to the upper chest or base of neck. You will not be able to handle as much weight using this form as you did in workout #1, but the pump will be far greater.

(2) Incline lying triceps extensions, 3 x 12-15 reps

Form: Nothing fancy here – use the same form as in workout #1.

Biceps:

(1) Standing straight-bar curls, 3x12-15 reps

Form: Use a grip slightly wider than shoulder width as opposed to the narrower grip of workout #1.

(2) Seated incline dumbell curls, 3 x 12-15 reps

Form: Same as in workout #1.

Workout #3: Supersetting

Biceps/triceps:

(1) Straight-bar curls supersetted with close-grip bench presses, 3 x 8-10 reps

Form: same as in workout #I for both exercises.

(2) Incline curls supersetted with incline lying triceps extensions, 3 x 8-10 reps

Form: same as in workout #1.

Workout #4: The Nonworkout

This is a trick I have seen many people use in order to avoid overtraining and kick-start their arms into renewed growth. It was a particular favorite of muscle monster Mike Francois

Midpoint   *Finish*

Tom Platz gives new meaning to the word *intensity* on alternate dumbell curls. *Start*

Finish

(see "Large and in Charge" in issue 144 of *MuscleMag International* for more info), who at one time was having difficulty adding size to his arms – if you can believe that!

On this rotation you drop arms from the training regimen and start back again the next time arms would come up in your workout split. For example, if you normally do chest and arms together you would do only chest, then add arms back in the following week when chest day comes around again. I have used this trick many times with my clients, and it rarely fails to help them add new size and strength to their arms. Remember, your arms are being worked quite adequately with your chest and back workouts, so don't be afraid to neglect them for a week. Get the best results by taking advantage of this technique.

Conclusion

You will notice I have put biceps-training and triceps-training together in one workout. Some bodybuilders have great success splitting them up with other bodyparts. However, for the person who is having trouble adding new size to his/her arms (the proverbial hard gainer), I have seen better results when they are done together. I can't go down the list here, but I have interviewed and/or trained many successful amateur and pro bodybuilders who told me that when they started doing biceps and triceps together in the same workout, their arms began growing again. I don't have a scientific explanation for this phenomenon, but more often than not it appears to be the case. I suspect it probably has to do with neurological factors and increased blood flow to the area, but who knows – or cares – for that matter? As for which bodypart you should do with arms (chest, back or shoulders), that decision is really up to you. I prefer to do my arms with my chest, but plenty of people will do arms with back or shoulders, or even alone on a separate day.

This program (workouts #1,2,3 and the nonworkout) should take you four weeks, assuming you are working arms once per week, and I would not recommend doing them more often. At the end of the nonworkout (I don't call it a break so your friends won't call you a wimp), you would start with workout #I and go through the cycle again. You should do this until you get bored with it, which is usually four or five cycles. At that point you can drop the seated incline dumbell curls and replace them with preacher curls. Drop lying extensions for triceps cable pushdowns. Do several more cycles until you get bored, and then go back to the original program. This should keep you busy – and I hope growing – for a long time so you won't stray away from the productive arm exercises because of boredom, and end up doing one-arm cable curls till the cows come home with no results. You people who sent me those letters, and you know who you are, this arm workout is for you. For anyone else who is having trouble putting size on his arms, this program won't let you down.

Lee Priest

Chapter Sixteen

Why Are Bodybuilders So Afraid Of Change?

Some time ago I was sitting at the counter of the juice bar at my gym reading a muscle magazine when I noticed a young aspiring bodybuilder with a look of despair on his face. He looked as if someone had run over his dog after stealing his girlfriend. "What's the problem?" I inquired. "It's chest day, I have to bench and I hate to bench. That's the problem!" he retorted. "My bench press hasn't budged in months. I can't even get a pump from it." "So why bench at all?" I said. "Why not take a few months off from benching and do something completely different that might shock your muscles into new growth, or at least renew your enthusiasm for training?" To my surprise he looked at me as if I had just told him there was no Santa Claus, or that those steroid replacement kits you see in the magazines won't make you look like Lee Haney. He got up off his chair and walked away, not wanting to hear any more of my sacrilege. This experience got me to thinking. Are all bodybuilders as close minded and inflexible as this guy? No wonder so many of them fail to make any progress.

Matt McLaughlin

Bodybuilding is a sport of constant adaptation and change. The very definition of *adaptation* is "the ability of an individual or organism to adjust itself to different conditions, environments, etc." We have known for many years that the person or animal that can adapt the fastest to change is always the most successful. If a commercial enterprise fails to adapt to its customers' needs, it will continue to lose market share until it finally goes out of business. If an animal is unable to adjust to a changing environment, it will become extinct. If a bodybuilder fails to adapt to his body's ever-changing needs, he will fail to make any continued progress. Being inflexible does not lead just to boredom. It leads to extinction!

Good genetics aside, successful bodybuilders instinctively know when to change the aspects of their workout or diet that are not yielding the results they want, while retaining those aspects that continue to be beneficial. They might raise or lower their reps for a certain bodypart or all bodyparts, change their whole routine around, take a few days off, or just do something totally out of the ordinary to keep their training interesting. The point is, successful bodybuilders enjoy and look forward to their workouts. If they don't, they know something is wrong and it's time for a change. Meanwhile, we have people like that kid I talked to who thinks the rules of bodybuilding are carved in stone somewhere. Well, I am here to tell you they are not! There is not a missing eleventh commandment that reads "Thou shalt not avoid bench presses on chest day." Of course, there are general guidelines that are true, such as:

(1) The stronger you can make a muscle, the larger it will be.

(2) Compound movements are generally more productive than isolation movements for building mass.

Are there exceptions to these guidelines? You bet your big squatter's butt there are! Here's an example. If you put only 60 percent of your usual intensity into squats because you are so damned sick of doing them but put 110 percent intensity into leg extensions because its been a long time since you did them, the leg extensions will be more productive. The same idea would apply to bench presses and incline flyes. If you're not enjoying a particular exercise any more, regardless of how productive it used to be (i.e. the law of diminishing returns), you will be unable to put 100 percent of your effort into it. Enjoyment leads to enthusiasm. Enthusiasm leads to harder workouts. Harder workouts lead to growth. Don't be afraid to try something new if it will increase your enthusiasm, thus increasing the productivity of your workouts.

Throughout this book I have stressed that you should stick to the basic multijoint movements – and you should – but there is always that occasion when you need to do something different to have a little fun or get the old flame burning again. This last chapter on training is just a few workouts for you to try, and a few ideas that I hope will lead to a bit more enjoyment from your workouts if you are feeling a little stale. Obviously you should be changing your routine every two to three months. When was the last time you changed it? For example, go into the gym one day and do your set routine backwards for no reason. Instead of doing thighs and hamstrings, start off with hamstrings. Instead of doing shoulders and arms, start with arms and then do shoulders.

Back in college every Saturday was road-trip day. My training partner and I would look up a new gym in the phone book, pack the car with food and take off. We would drive up to

Roland Kickinger

three hours to a new gym, but we always had a great workout. It never failed to inspire us to train harder. What a great way to keep the dreaded training rut away. I remember reading somewhere that Arnold Schwarz-a-money-maker once filled his car with weights and drove out to the country with his partner to work out in the woods. I tried that too – it was a blast! Have you ever done preacher curls over a tree stump? What a pump!

Below are a couple of ideas you can try for each bodypart just to kick some life into your workouts. They are not based on latest scientific research, or some Mr. So and So's championship workout, but they are designed to cause a killer pump, some renewed enthusiasm and a broad smile.

The Five-Minute Chest Routine

This was a routine Mike Mentzer recommended a while back. (I don't know if he still does it). Done correctly, it's a real killer. If you have limited time or just want to try something totally new, this is a routine for you. I must warn you though that it can cause extreme soreness the following day. If you do it right, it should take about five minutes. Do not rest at all between these exercises (run from machine to machine if you have to), and you must go to absolute failure on each set.

(1) Pec-dek: one and one-quarter reps, l x 12
(2) Flat-bench press to neck: 10 reps to failure; strip off some weight and continue till failure; strip off more weight and continue till failure again. (one set with a total of three stripdowns)
(3) Negative dips: l x 12. Put a weight in your belt and do negative reps. Descend slowly. Then jump up and descend again until 12 reps are completed.
(4) Pushups: l x 15 plus negatives. After the negative dips jump immediately to the floor and do pushups till failure. When you reach failure, continue on with 8 to 10 negatives.

Back Triset From Hell

Three trisets of weighted chinups, deadlifts and straight-arm pushdowns: Keep the chinups in the 10-to-12 rep range, the deadlifts around 8 to 10 reps, and the straight-arm pushdowns 15+ reps. You don't have to jump from station to station, though this workout does not take long. Take a few breaths between sets. Don't forget to warm up thoroughly before you start.

Super Shoulder Burner

Rear laterals, side laterals, front raises and presses: Take a pair of dumbells and start with bent-over laterals. Use a weight with which you reach failure at about 12 reps. When you can do no more, immediately stand up and continue with side laterals until failure. When you die on the side laterals, start the front raises. Do this cycle three times. After the lateral cycle, finish off with 2 sets of seated barbell military presses – if you are able to raise your arms above your head!

Quad/Hamstring Terminators

Three giant sets of leg extensions (12 to 15 reps), squats (8 to 10 reps), leg presses (12 to 15 reps) and straight-leg deadlifts (10 to 12 reps): Three giant sets are a total of 12 sets for legs. You had better be close to the bathroom or keep a garbage can close by for this one!
OR
(1) Leg extensions: 8 sets of 12 to 15 reps.
(2) Squats: 2 sets of 15 to 20 reps.
(3) Leg curls supersetted with straight-leg deadlifts: 3 supersets of 10 to 15 reps. This workout will cause a pump and burn that will last for days.

Arms and Calves

I won't go into great detail about arms. They are a small muscle group and are fairly straightforward to train. Most people fail to make gains in their arms because of chronic overtraining (see chapter 15), loose form, bad genetics, inadequate calorie intake, or a combination of all four possible factors. Try reducing the sets, lightening up the weight, cleaning up the form and using the routines from chapter 15. You see a lot of guys and gals in the gym on an arm day working every muscle in their body except arms. Their form is that bad! Don't waste your time being one of these people.

Although calves are considered to be a small muscle, there is nothing straightforward about training them unless you happen to be one of those rare people who were born with great calves which seem to grow no matter what you do. For the 99 percent of the world who have to almost kill themselves trying to possess a respectable pair of calves, chapter 14 will be just what the doctor ordered.

Conclusion

This is just the tip of the iceberg for strategies that are useful for getting the old fires burning and adding some renewed enthusiasm to your workouts. Sometimes we overintellectualize a thing to death, or take life just a little too seriously, so that we lose all the fun of an activity that should bring us enjoyment. Many professional bodybuilders have found out the hard way that working out was no longer enjoyable after it became a job. Even if you are not a professional bodybuilder, it is easy to let your workouts feel more like a job than an enjoyable activity. When that happens, it usually is time to try something new, change the routine, or take some time off from the gym.

These exercises and recommendations are not intended to be followed every workout, but added in occasionally to shock the body and keep the mind interested. Try adding one of these workouts into your routine for one body-part per week for a change of pace. Take a road trip. Train naked (just kidding!). I can assure you that there is not a single top amateur or professional bodybuilder who is not constantly

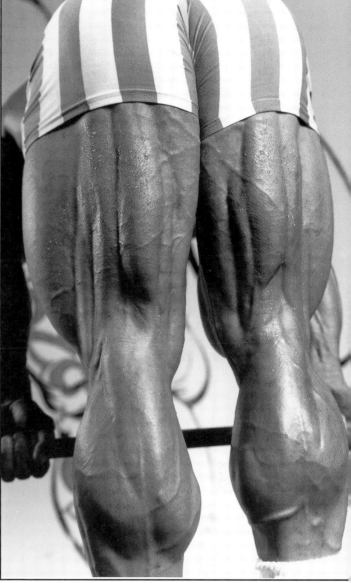

These outrageous hamstrings belong to top pro Michael Francois.

learning and constantly changing (i.e. adapting) his approach to gaining muscle. It is one of many factors – besides superior genetics – that set successful athletes apart from the crowd. Inflexibility is a sign of a closed mind. If you want a skinny body and a closed mind that's your business, but if muscle is what you seek, an open mind and a willingness to try something new are essential.

Finish

Start

Craig Titus works his rear delts with bent-over laterals.

Chapter Seventeen

The Best and Worst Bodybuilding Has To Offer

Anja Schreiner and Sharon Bruneau

It is easy to lose sight of the important things in life. We can get caught up in all the advertising glitz, supplement wars, bodybuilding shows, back-stabbing and rumor-mongering, and lose sight of why we love to lift weights in the first place. If there were no contests, no supplement companies touting miracles, and no money to be made, would you still lift weights? I know the answer for me, and I hope for you, is a resounding yes! Bodybuilding makes you feel better physically and mentally. It is the single best method of exercise there is for your health, and doing it makes you look kind of cool too. Unfortunately, like any lifestyle or sport, bodybuilding can either be one of the most positive influences in a person's life, or it can create a life filled with negative behavior leading to disastrous results.

The Best Bodybuilding Has To Offer

Dr. Dullnig was a physician with AIDS. He wrote a column in each issue of *Muscle Media 2000* under the moniker "Dr. X," chronicling his experience as an AIDS victim with an honesty, humor and wit you rarely find in a person living under such circumstances. With his health quickly failing, and no help in sight from the medical community, Dr. Dullnig found bodybuilding. Through weight training, a high-quality/high-protein diet, and, yes, those "evil" steroids, he brought his health back to almost what it once was. He summed his experience up well in his last column: "The medical community didn't help me with this. The AIDS community didn't help me with this. The gay community didn't help me with this. Even my closest friends didn't help me with this. Nobody I knew, knew anything to help me. But the bodybuilders knew something, and I translated that into something fantastic for me."

He shared his experiences with the virus and steroids honestly and openly. He demonstrated that anabolic steroids, combined with weight training, were extremely effective at reversing the muscle-wasting and immune suppression of the AIDS virus. He was extremely critical of the medical community for its approach (or lack of) to this disease, and its disinterest in using steroids in the treatment of AIDS patients. He had found a partial answer to the management of AIDS, and wanted to share this information with everyone he could.

Dr. Dullnig did not want to win any trophies. He did not want to make any money or endorse supplements. He just wanted to live. Through the wonderful lifestyle that is bodybuilding, he was able to extend the quality and quantity of his life far longer than would have otherwise been possible. In essence, in spirit and in practice, Dr. Dullnig demonstrated what is truly important in life: life itself! Not trophies, not money, not magazine covers, not a 20-inch arm, but a higher quality of life, which weight training and a good diet can deliver to anyone, regardless of who you are. Young or old, sick or healthy, male or female, bodybuilding can improve your health, your appearance and your self-image – and that is its own reward.

Because of a serious medical condition that arose, Dr. Dullnig had to stop using steroids. His health quickly failed. His condition became intolerable to him, and he took his own life. But Dr. Dullnig did not die in vain. His research, and the resulting book he started, could benefit the lives of millions of people. Through his column he probably helped hundreds or thousands of AIDS sufferers.

Sometimes a story such as this is necessary to show us what is really important. Don't ever lose sight of it. I don't know about you, but the experience of Dr. Dullnig gives me a far greater appreciation of the meager weights that I (in comparison to some 300-pound monster) get to lift in good health each day. I am certainly into the business of bodybuilding as much as anyone could be, and I love the sport aspect of bodybuilding as much as anyone, but I always try to keep in perspective what is really important, and I hope you will try to do the same.

The Worst Bodybuilding Has To Offer

The road to despair, depression and personal destruction is a complex one. The media and many misinformed medical professionals have blown the whole steroid issue so far out of proportion and reality that no one knows who to listen to any more. Steroids do not make ax murderers out of normal people. Nor do they cause your penis to fall off or horns to grow from your head. Can they have serious side effects? Absolutely! If you have ever read the story of Steve Michalik in *The Village Voice* ("The Power and the Gory" by Paul Solotaroff), you know that it described steroid abuse at its worst. However, anyone who knows anything about bodybuilding realized that story had more holes in it than a mouse shot with a 12-gauge.

The author of the article took considerable liberty with his artistic license (which should be revoked) in writing that piece. Where the truth starts and the sensationalism ends is unclear. If even a fraction of that article were true, it's no place you ever want to find yourself. The only part that was truly interesting – or relevant – in that article was Steve's account of how his father was so abusive to him as child that he grew up with severe emotional problems regarding his self-worth as a man and human being. To make up for his intense feelings of inferiority, he turned to steroids and ultimately abused them to the point that his health was in serious jeopardy. Hey, many kids, including me, started lifting weights because being skinny made them feel a bit insecure. It is the intensity of these feelings, that don't go away no matter how big the person gets, that leads to the type of drug abuse Mr. Michalik experienced – almost a reverse anorexia.

Section Five – Last Comments

We shouldn't need a scare story of dubious information to tell us people are abusing drugs – all kinds of drugs – as a result of severe emotional troubles. Believe me, the majority of bodybuilders who get themselves into physical trouble from drugs are using a lot more than just steroids. Cocaine, marijuana, tobacco, Nubain and alcohol, to name but a common few, are also part of the problem. Their emotional troubles usually began long before their physical problems. The fact is, steroids are probably one of the most benign drugs a person could pick to abuse, but any drug can kill you if taken in large enough dosages for long enough periods of time. If you are a competitive athlete who uses moderate amounts of steroids, works with a doctor and regularly gets blood tests, that's your business and I pass no moral judgment on you. If you take huge amounts of steroids to mask your feelings of inferiority, anger, shame, etc., you have embraced the worst bodybuilding has to offer and you had better take a close look in the mirror. Your choice does not make you a bad person, just a mortal one like the rest of us.

Lee Priest

Conclusion

I did not want to make this last chapter depressing. The truth is, bodybuilding is one of the most healthful endeavors you can undertake for both your body and mind. Legal, moral and ethical issues aside, steroids can have positive effects, as they did for Dr. Dullnig, and negative effects, as they did for Mr. Michalik. Unless you have a medical reason for using steroids – and there are many legitimate medical applications for these drugs – or you are a professional bodybuilder, I recommend you stay away from anabolics altogether.

Adding muscle to your frame always improves your self-image, but it should not be the modulator of your self-esteem. You will not be less of a person with less muscle, only a smaller version (yipes!). Conversely, you will not be a better person with more muscle, only a larger version of your former self. Use the bodybuilding lifestyle as it was intended – to achieve a higher quality of life.

Best of luck in all your bodybuilding endeavors.

Will Brink

Ian Harrison

Index

Photo Index

Contributing Photographers
Jim Amentler, Garry Bartlett,
Ralph DeHaan, Irvin Gelb,
Robert Kennedy, Chris Lund,
Jason Mathas, Mitsuru Okabe.